Burlington Ontario in Colour Photos, Saving Our History One Photo at a Time

Photography
by Barbara Raué
2014

Series Name:
Cruising Ontario

Book 61: Burlington

Cover photo: Lakeshore Road

Series Name: Cruising Ontario
Saving Our History One Photo at a Time

Photos in full colour
Check the Appendixes in the back of each book for
descriptions of architectural terms and building styles

Book 33: Southampton
Book 34: Jarvis
Book 35: Hagersville
Book 36: Caledonia
Book 37: Simcoe
Book 38: Cambridge Part 1 – Galt Book 1
Book 39: Cambridge Part 1 – Galt Book 2
Book 40: Cambridge Part 2 – Preston
Book 41: Cambridge Part 3 – Hespeler
Book 42: Kitchener Book 1
Book 43: Kitchener Book 2
Book 46: Shelburne
Book 47: Alton, Mono and Caledon
Book 48: London in Colour
Book 50: Orangeville Beginnings in Colour
Book 51: Orangeville on Broadway in Colour
Book 52: Orangeville Book 3 in Colour
Book 53: Dundas in Colour Book 1
Book 54: Dundas in Colour Book 2
Book 55: Dundas in Colour Book 3
Book 56: Stratford
Book 57: Hanover
Book 58: New Hamburg Book 1
Book 59: New Hamburg Book 2 and Haysville
Book 60: Waterdown in Colour
Book 61: Burlington in Colour

Other Books by Barbara Raue

Coins of Gold

Arrows, Indians and Love

The Life and Times of Barbara
Volume 1: Inventions That Have Enhanced My Life
Volume 2: Entertainment That I Have Enjoyed
Volume 3: East Coast Trips
Volume 4: Olympics Have Always Intrigued Me
Volume 5: Wonders of the World
Volume 6: Caribbean Cruises We Have Enjoyed
Volume 7: Animals
Volume 8: Storms and Other Major Disasters in My Lifetime
Volume 9: Wars, Terrorist Attacks and Major Disasters

The Cromwell Family Book

In 1669 Rene-Robert de Cavelier de La Salle set out on the first of his many journeys of exploration intent on reaching the Ohio River, finding a way to the Southern Sea and thereby the route to China. Accompanied by the Sulpician missionaries Dollier and Gallinee, he left Montreal in July and reached Burlington Bay at the head of Lake Ontario two months later. La Salle continued inland to Tinaouataoua, a Seneca hamlet midway between present-day Dundas and Brantford, where he met Adrien Jolliet, an explorer returning from a mission to the Great Lakes. La Salle decided not to proceed westward and returned to Montreal by 1670.

Burlington

Burlington is located at the western end of Lake Ontario, lying between the north shore of the lake and the Niagara Escarpment, north of Hamilton. Before pioneer settlement in the 19th century, the area was covered by old-growth forest and was home to various First Nations peoples. In 1792, John Graves Simcoe, the first lieutenant governor of Upper Canada, named the western end of Lake Ontario "Burlington Bay" after the town of Bridlington in Yorkshire, England. Land beside the bay was deeded to First Nations Captain Joseph Brant at the turn of the nineteenth century. With the completion of the local survey after the War of 1812, the land was opened for settlement. Early farmers prospered because of the fertile soil and moderate temperatures. Lumber from the surrounding forests was a thriving business. In the latter half of the nineteenth century, local farmers switched to fruit and vegetable production. The first peaches grown in Canada were cultivated in the Grindstone Creek watershed in the south-west part of the city.

Hamilton Harbour, the western end of Lake Ontario, is bounded on its western shore by a large sandbar. A canal bisecting the sandbar allows ships access to Hamilton Harbour. The Burlington Bay James N. Allan Skyway, part of the Queen Elizabeth Way, and the Canal Lift Bridge allow access over the canal.

The leading industrial sectors are food processing, packaging, electronics, motor vehicle/transportation, business services, chemical/pharmaceutical and environmental.

Burlington is home to the Royal Botanical Gardens, which has the world's largest lilac collection.

Table of Contents

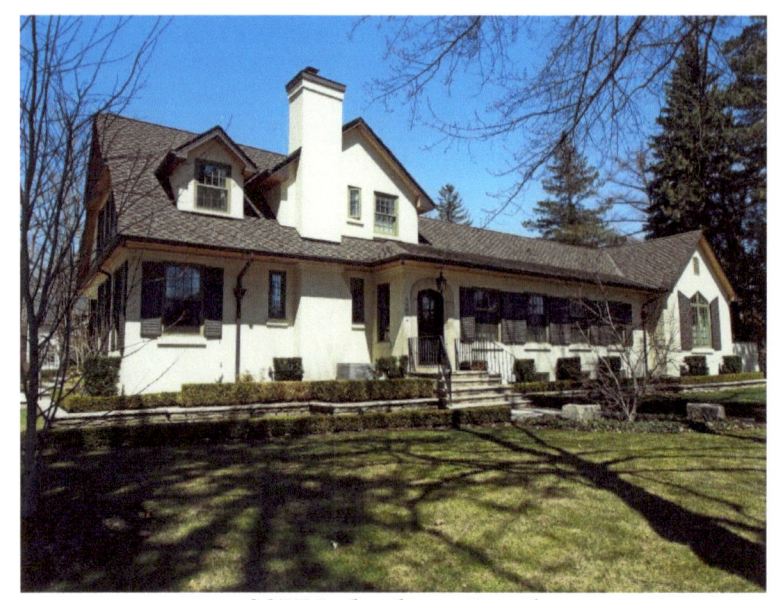
3057 Lakeshore Road

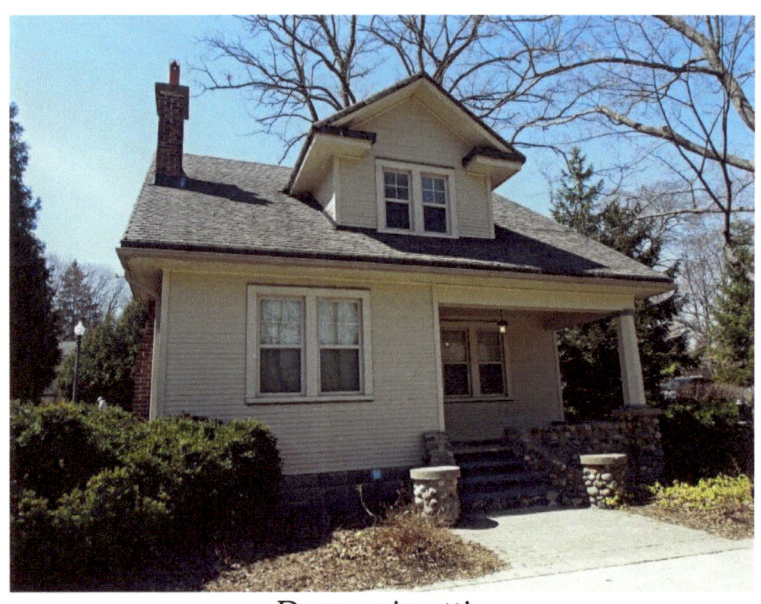
Dormer in attic

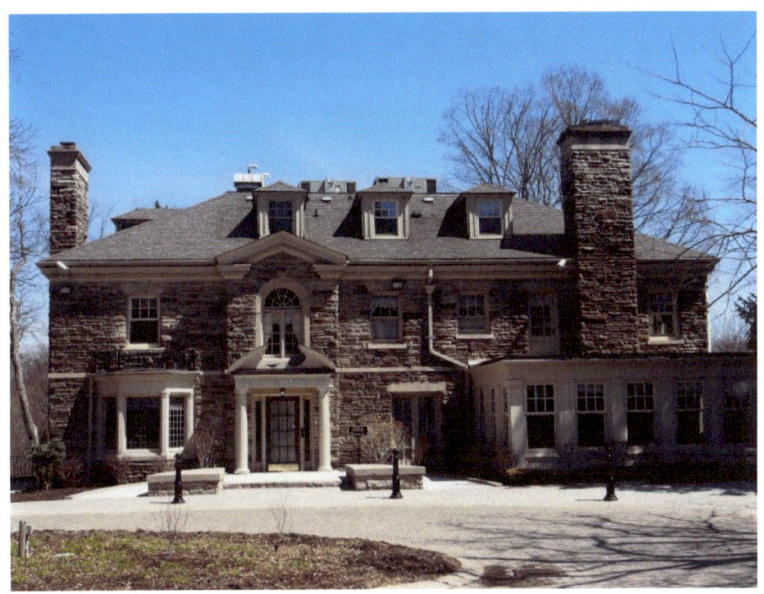

Paletta Mansion

Following the death of the prominent Hamilton industrialist
Cyrus Birge in 1929, his daughter Edythe MacKay used her
inheritance to replace the old Zimmerman farmhouse on her
Shore Acres Estate. It was built by local contractors and
craftsmen with the finest imported and local materials. In
1990 the City of Burlington purchased the estate for park
development. A fundraising campaign was carried out for the
restoration of the building and it was renamed in recognition
of a major donor, the Paletta family. It was restored and
renovated and reopened in 2000.

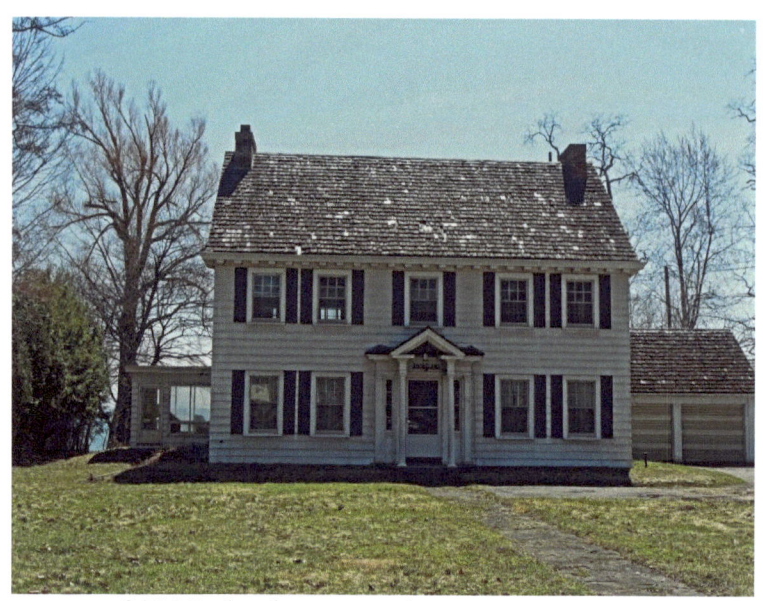

3050 Lakeshore Road – Georgian style

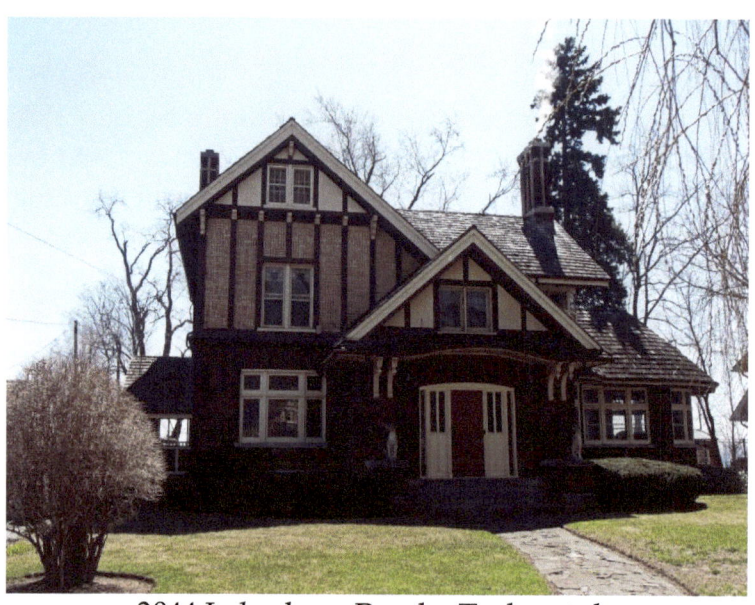

3044 Lakeshore Road – Tudor style

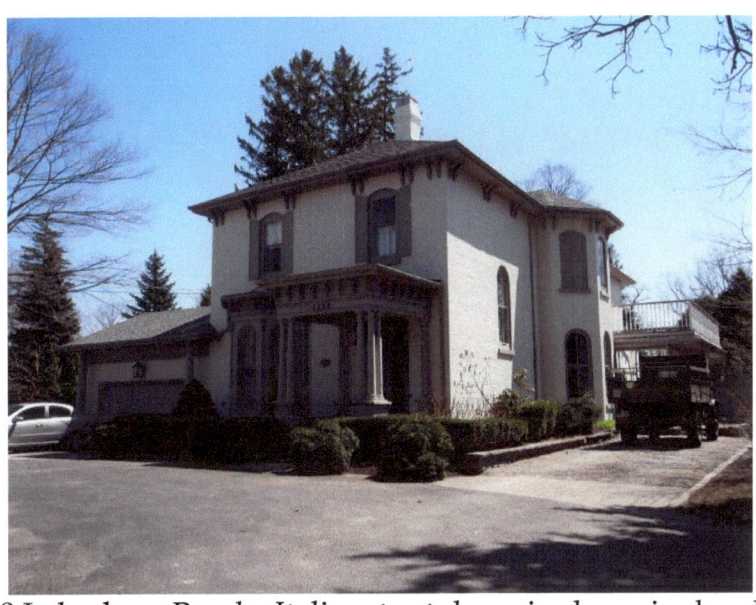

2230 Lakeshore Road – Italianate style, paired cornice brackets

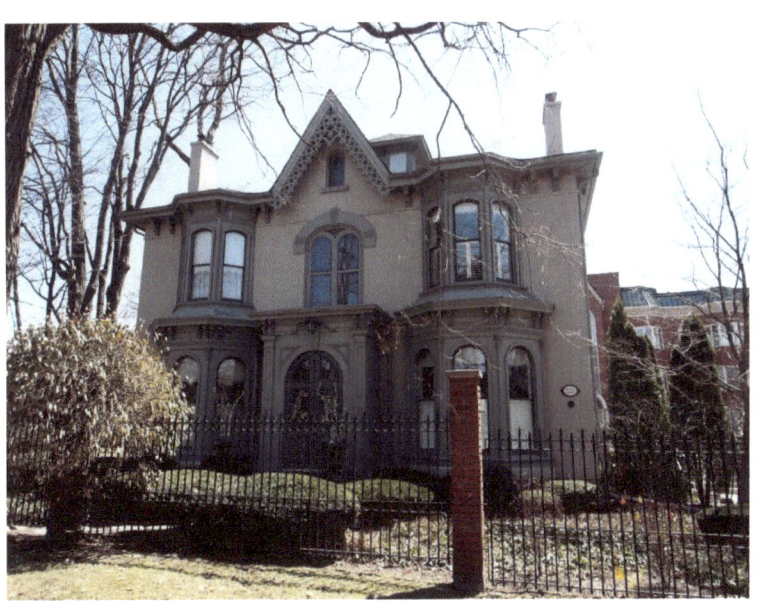

2222 Lakeshore Road – Italianate with two-and-a-half storey
tower-like bays with vergeboard trim on gable,
cornice brackets, dormer in roof

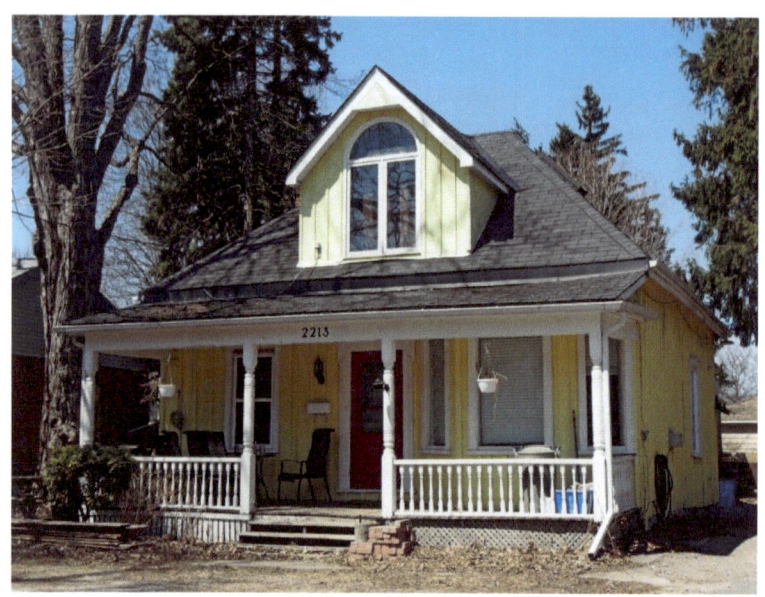

2213 Lakeshore Road - dormer

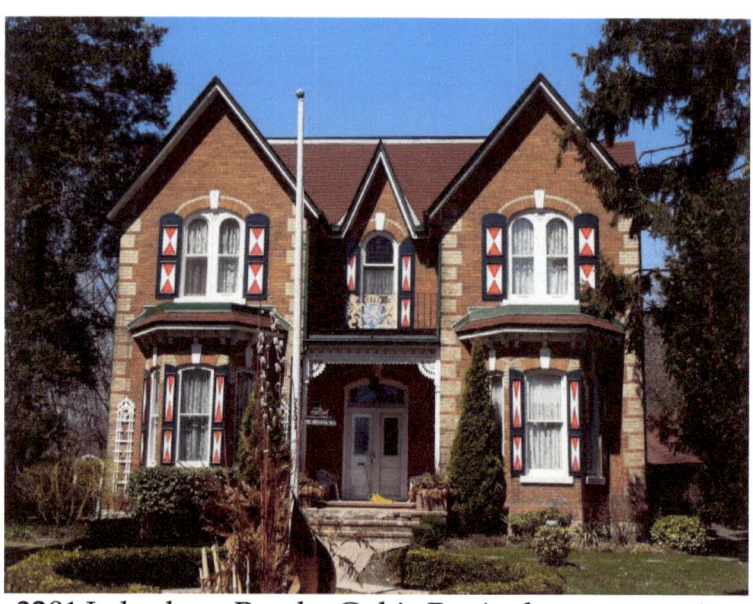

2201 Lakeshore Road – Gohic Revival, corner quoins

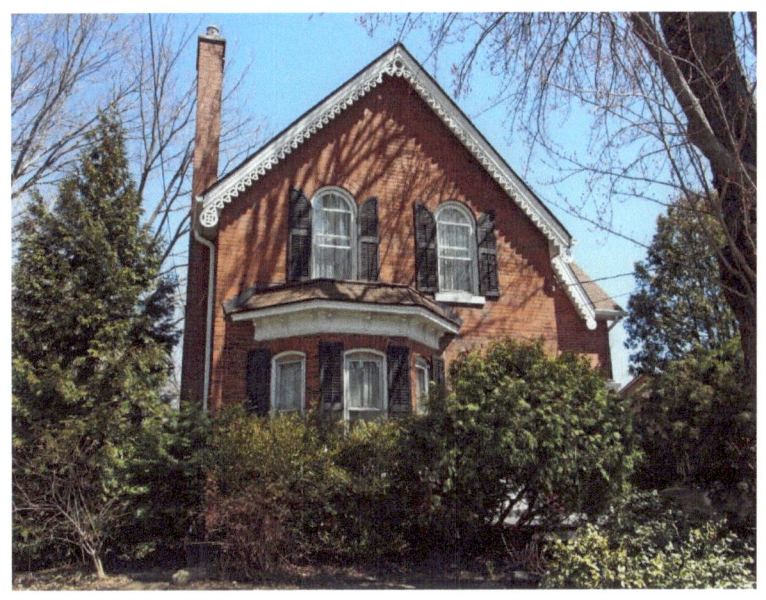

387 Lakeshore Road – Gothic Revival – vergeboard trim on gables, ground floor bay window

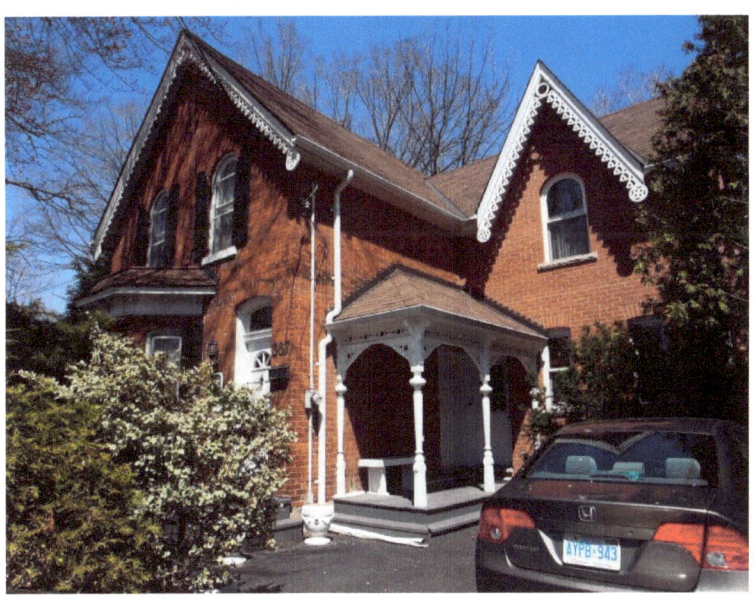

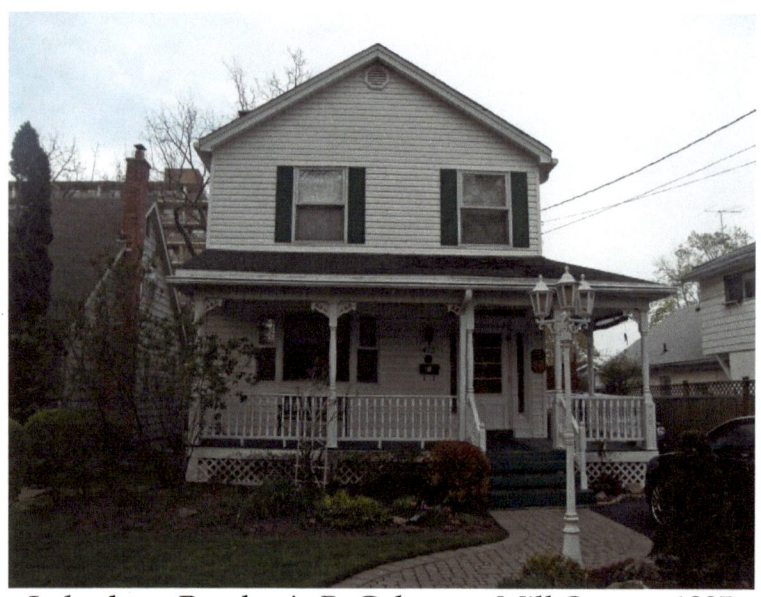

Lakeshore Road – A. B. Coleman, Mill Owner, 1895
Gothic Revival

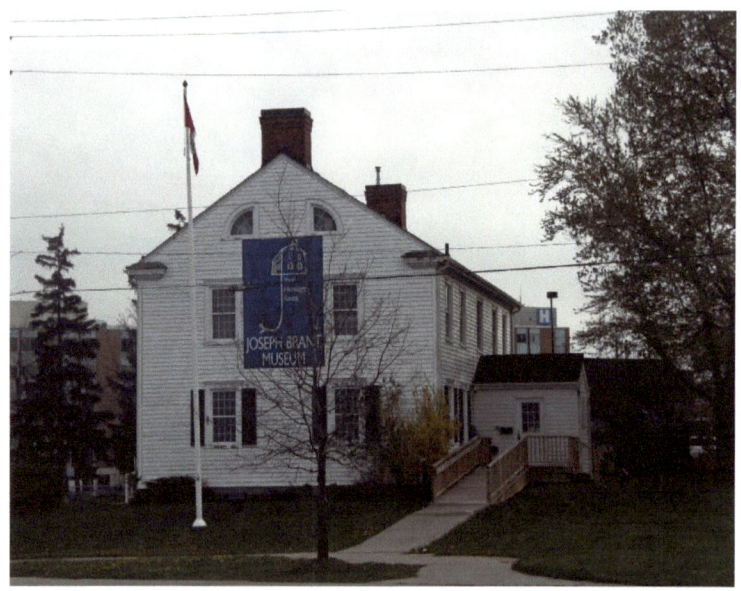

Lakeshore Road – Joseph Brant Museum

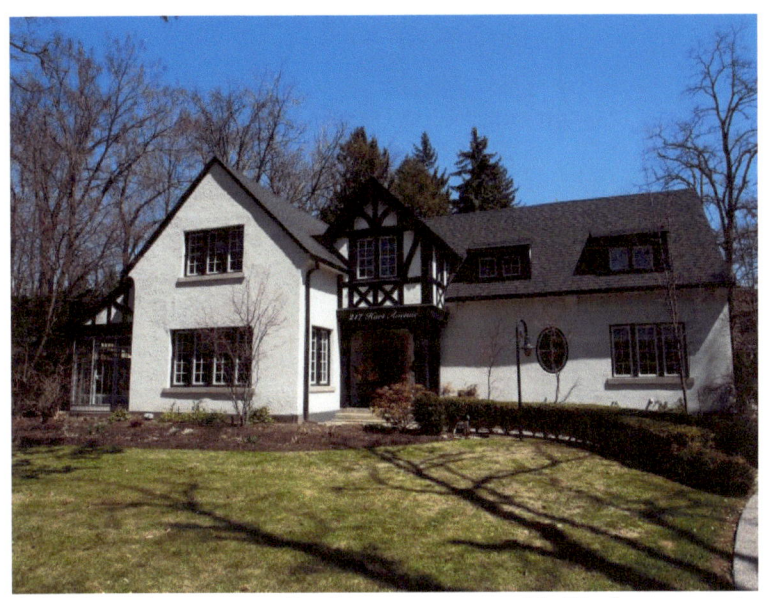

217 Hart Avenue – Gothic – stucco with Tudor accents

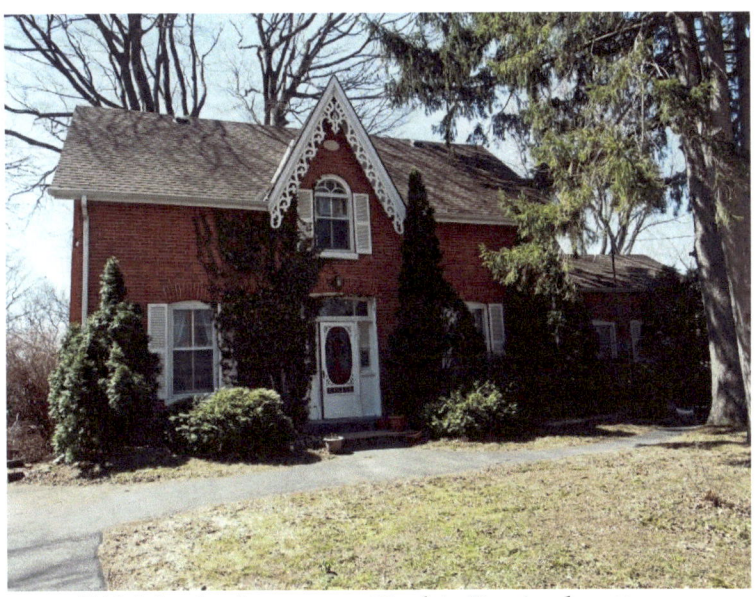

562 Maple Avenue – Gothic Revival cottage

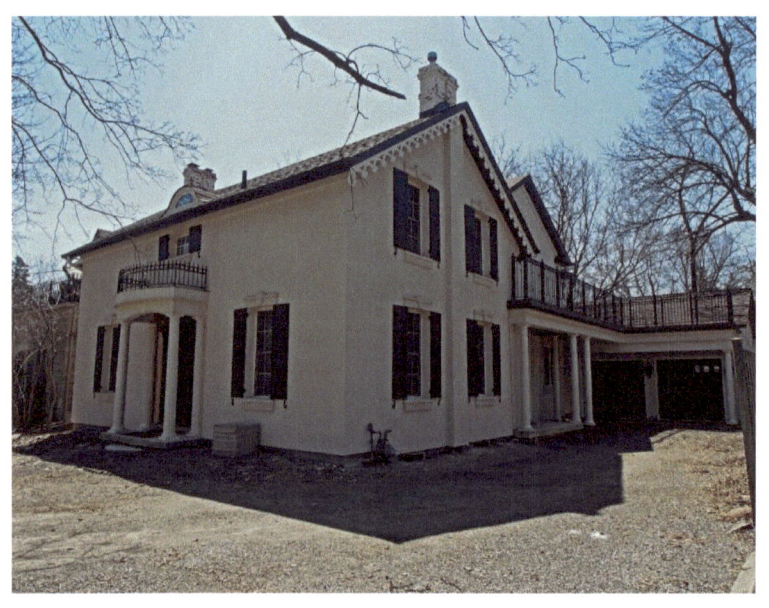

Guelph Line – Gothic Revival –bargeboard trim,
iron cresting above entrance

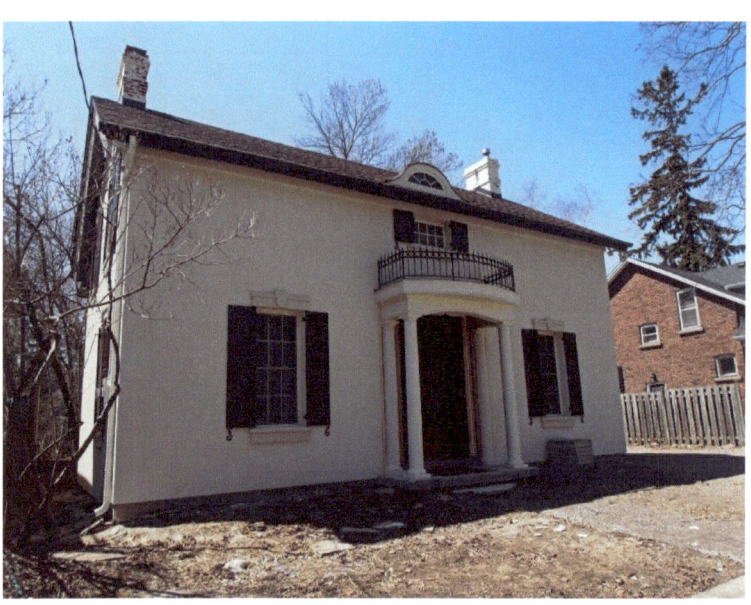

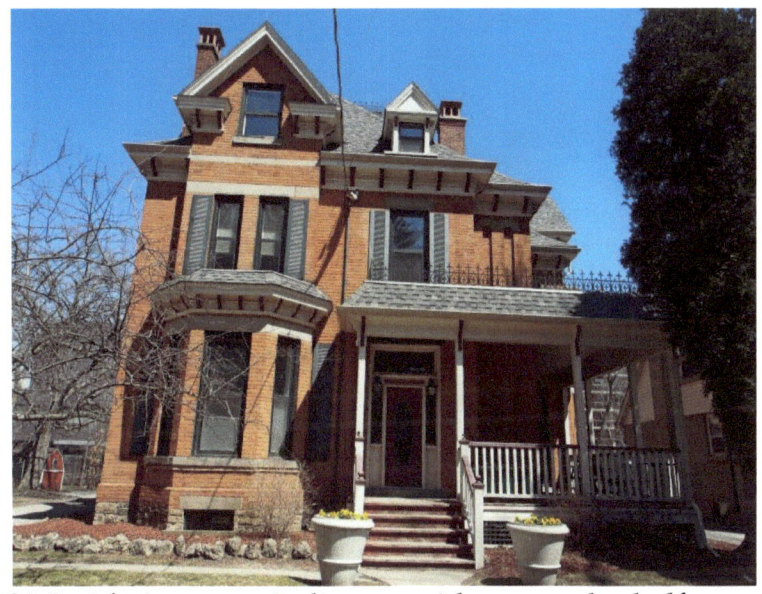

431 Smith Avenue – Italianate with two-and-a-half storey tower-like bay with cornice return on gable, dormer, single cornice brackets, bay window

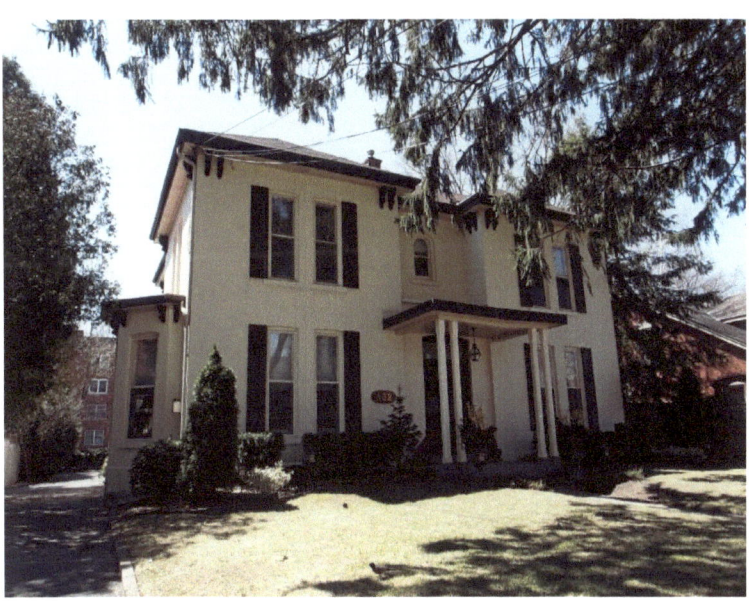

432 Smith Avenue – Italianate – paired cornice brackets

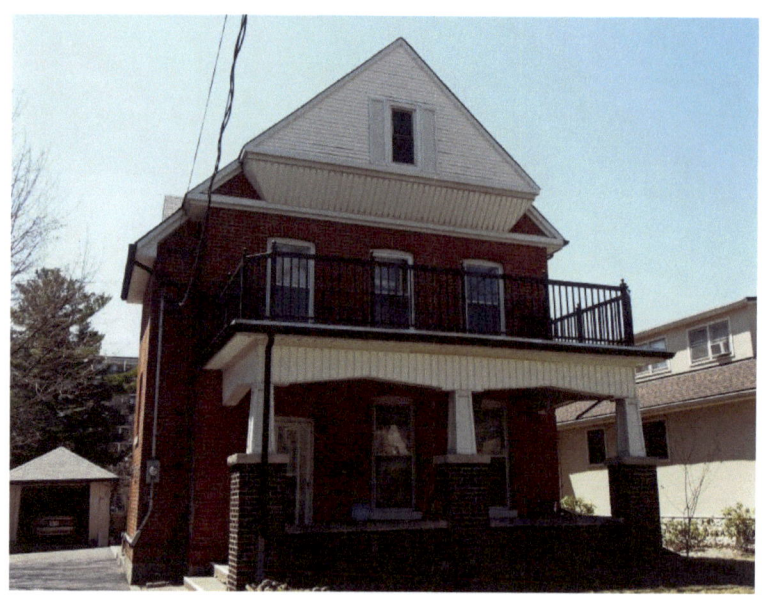

Smith Avenue

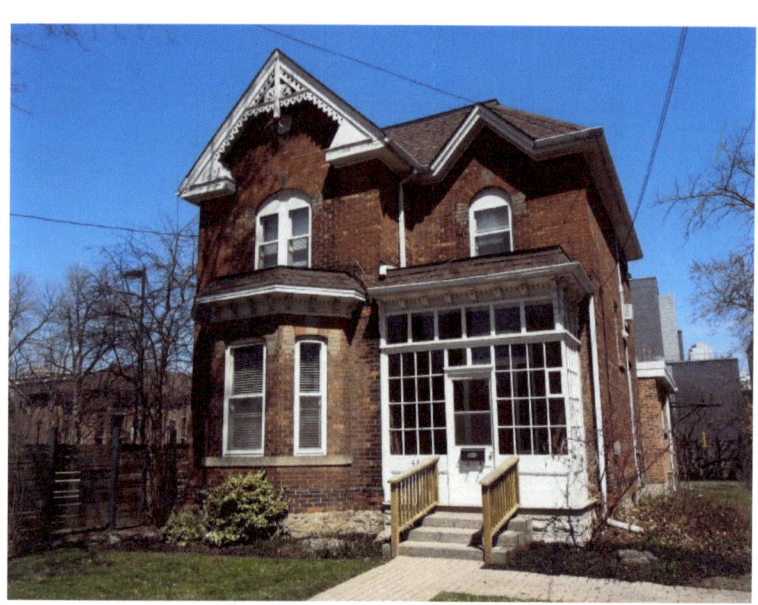

437 Smith Avenue – Italianate with Gothic gables, vergeboard trim, bay window with cornice brackets

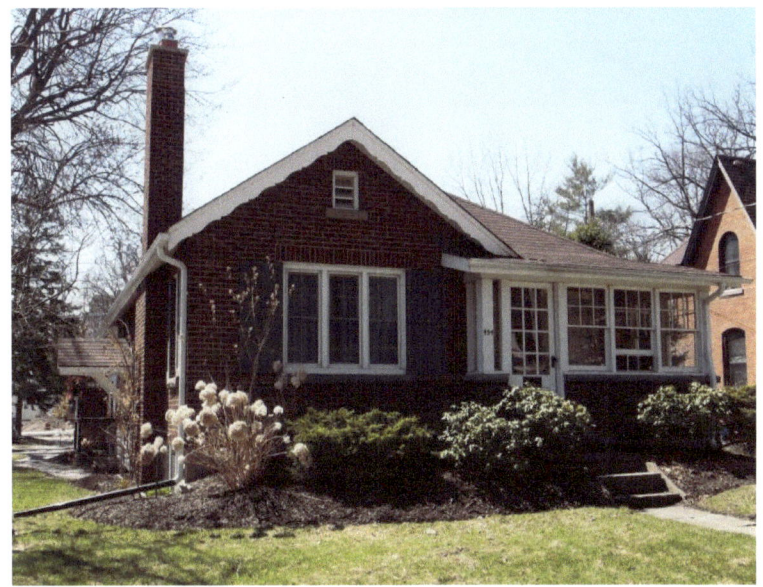

454 Burlington Avenue – one-and-a-half storey Gothic cottage

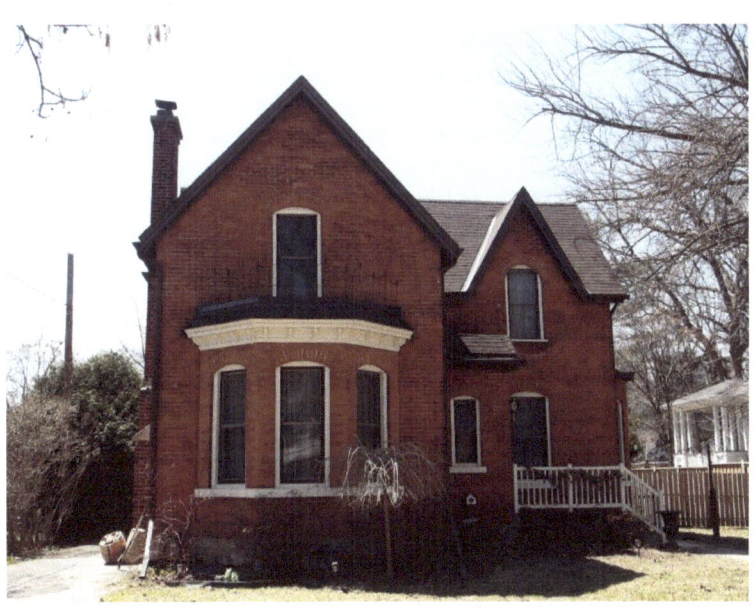

Burlington Avenue – Gothic Revival

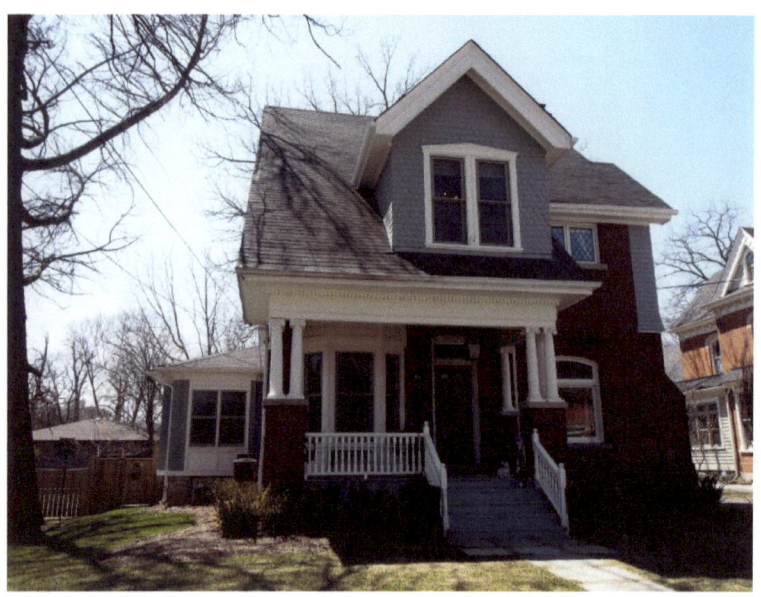

466 Burlington Avenue – Gothic Revival
with dormer above verandah

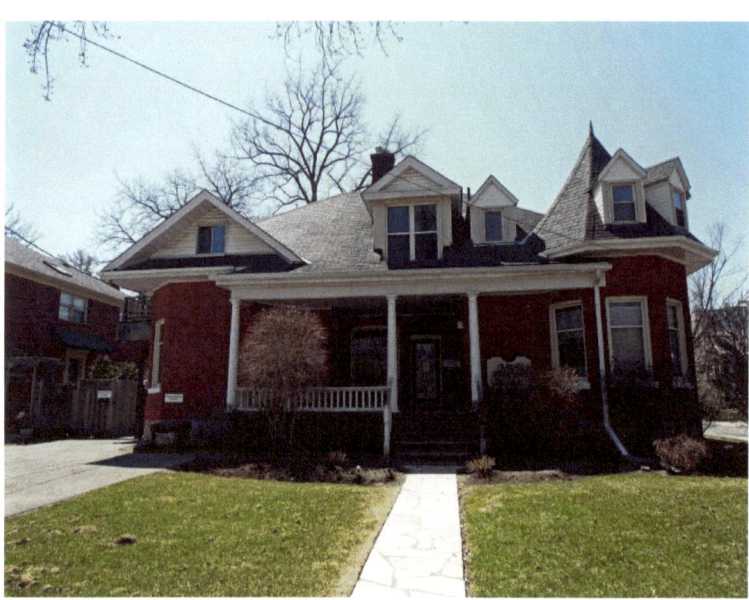

482 Burlington Avenue – Queen Anne style, dormers,
tower-like bay with cone-shaped roof

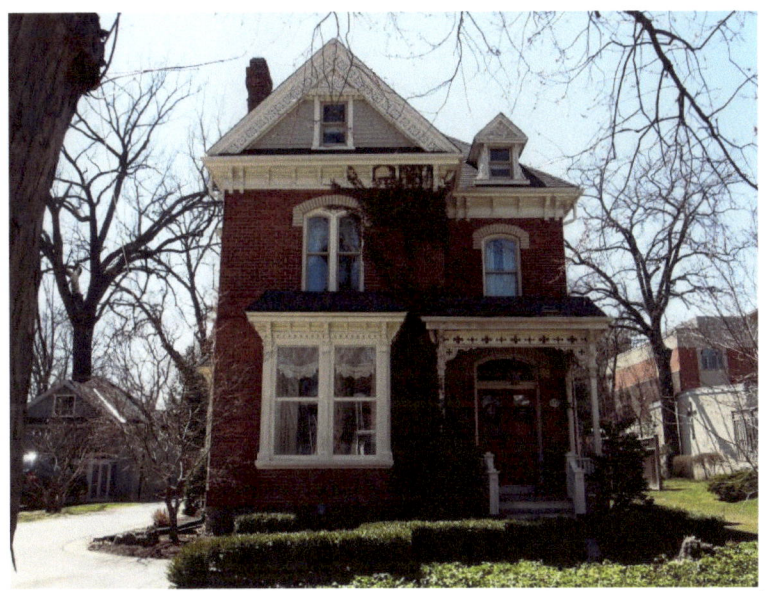

472 Burlington Avenue – Edwardian, dormer, cornice brackets

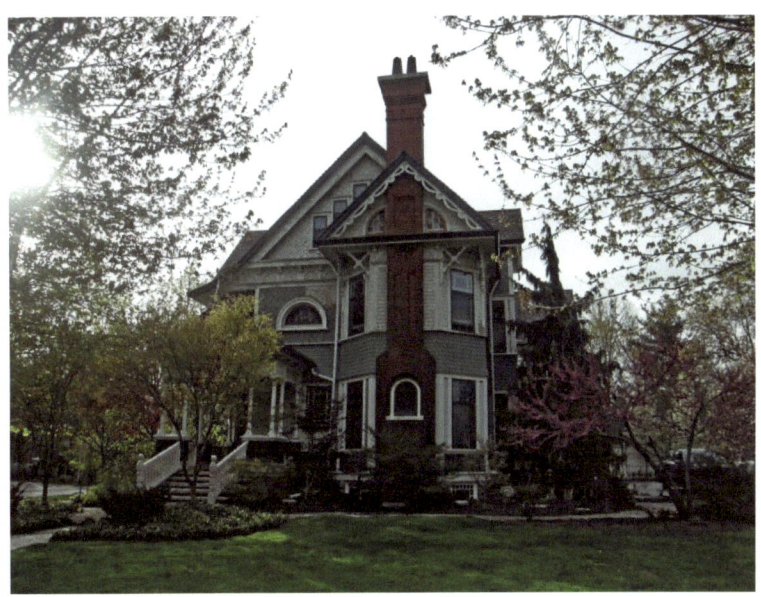

Burlington Avenue – Queen Anne – vergeboard trim,
decorative brickwork below cornice, half-moon window,
fish-scale pattern on tower

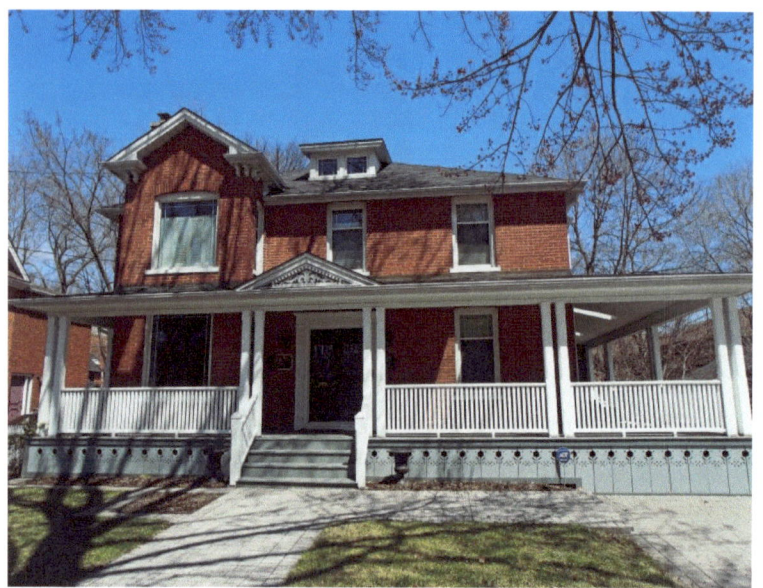

465 Burlington Avenue – Italianate with two-storey tower-like bay with cornice return on gable, dormer in attic, wrap-around verandah

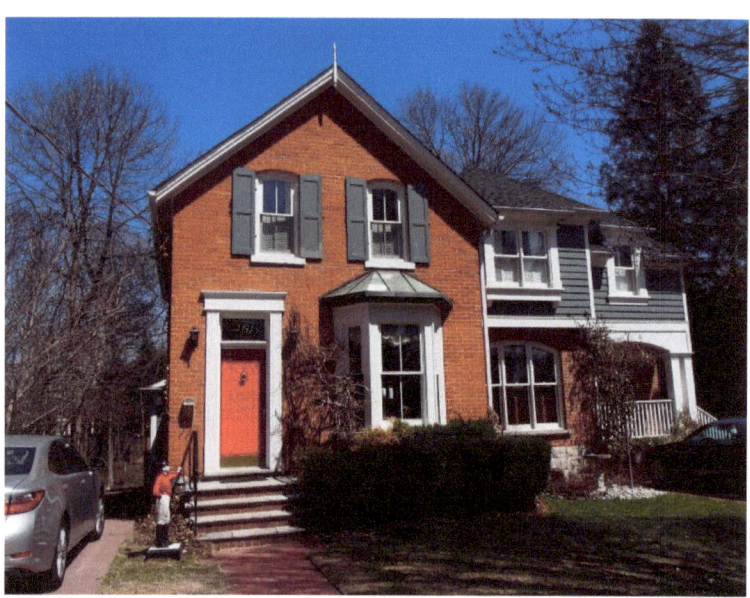

461 Burlington Avenue – Gothic Revival, finial on gable

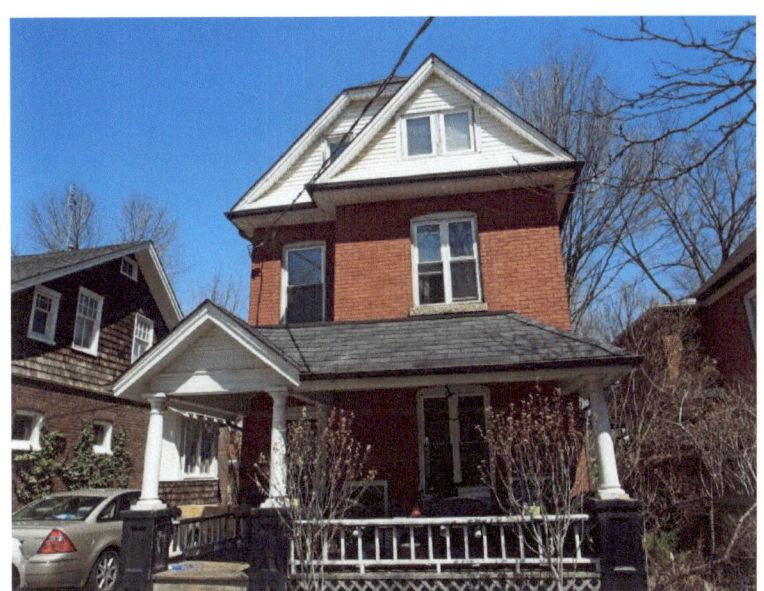

Burlington Avenue – Edwardian

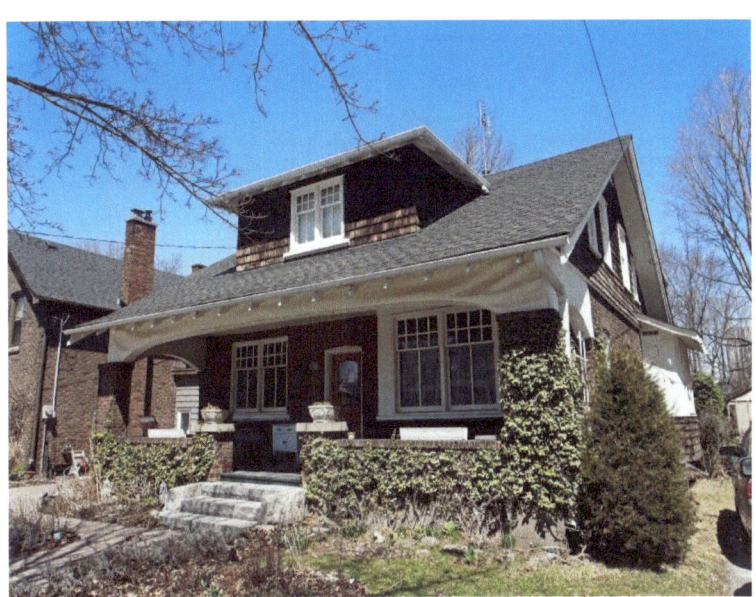

479 Burlington Avenue – Gothic Revival, dormer in attic,
deep cornice

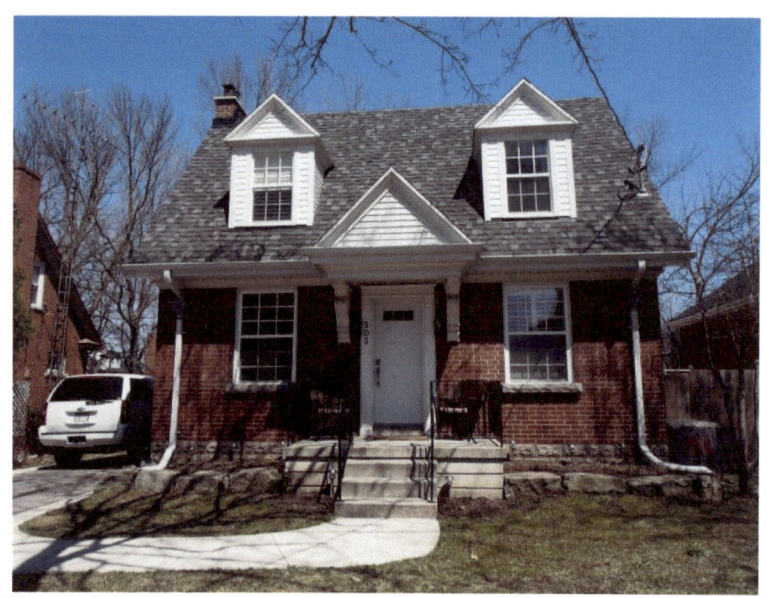

505 Burlington Avenue – Gothic Revival, dormers in attic, pediment above doorway

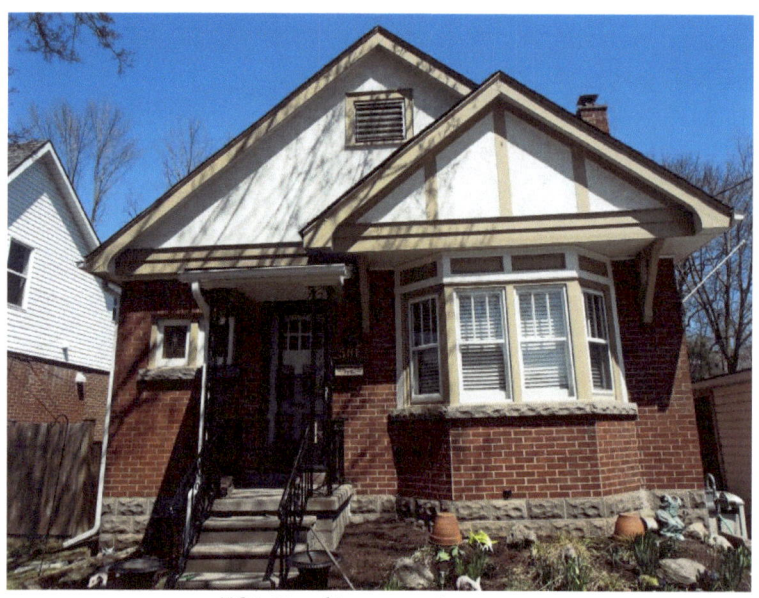

501 Burlington Avenue

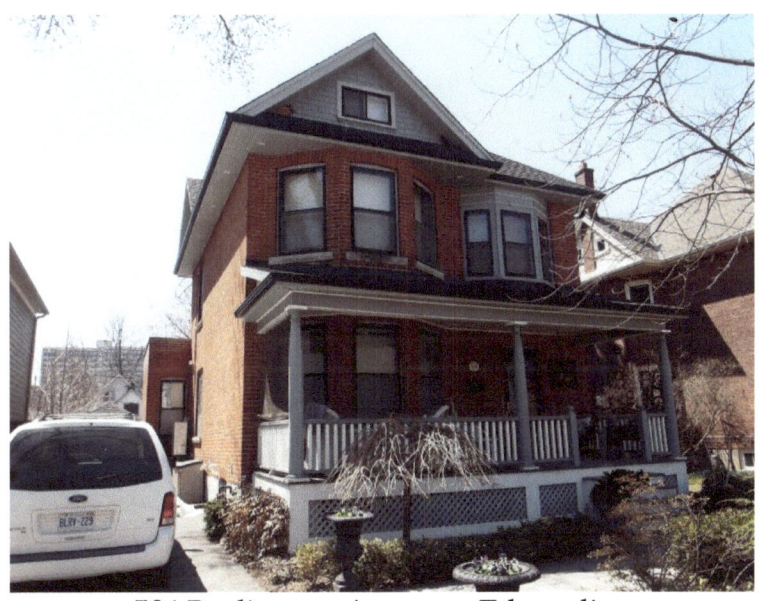

504 Burlington Avenue - Edwardian
Bay windows on second storey above verandah

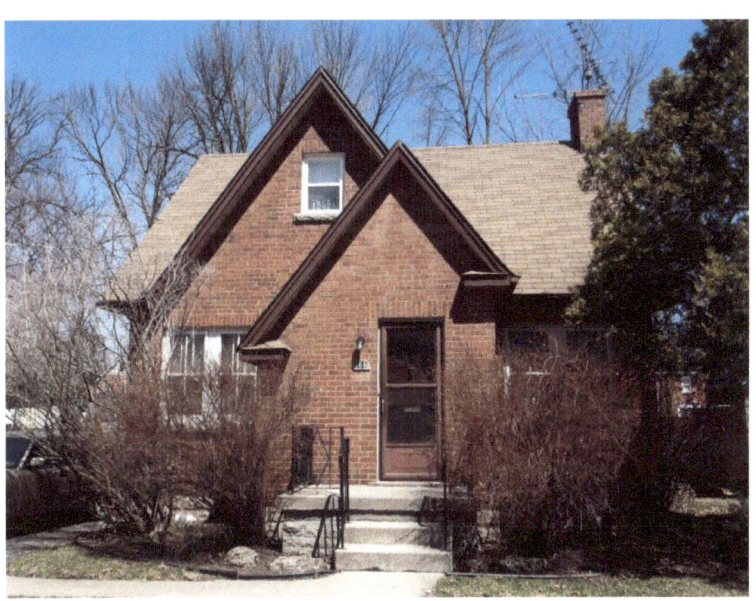

509 Burlington Avenue

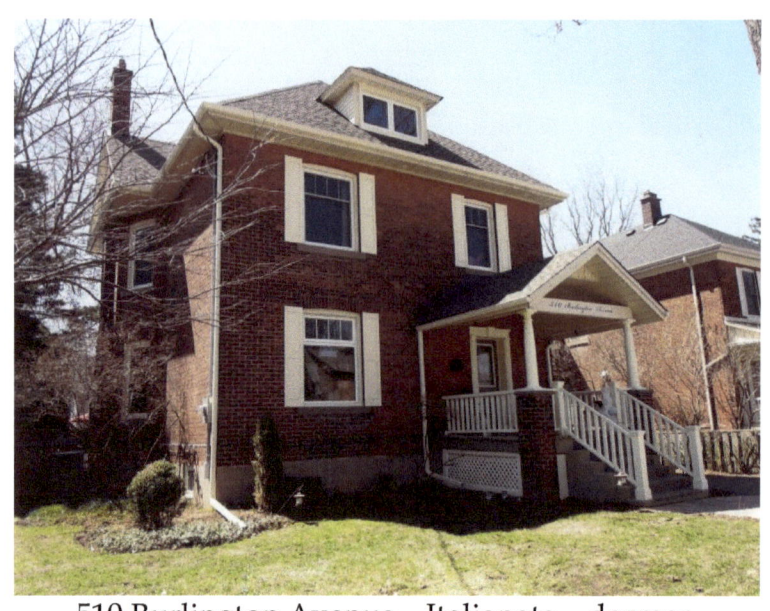

510 Burlington Avenue – Italianate – dormer,
pediment above porch

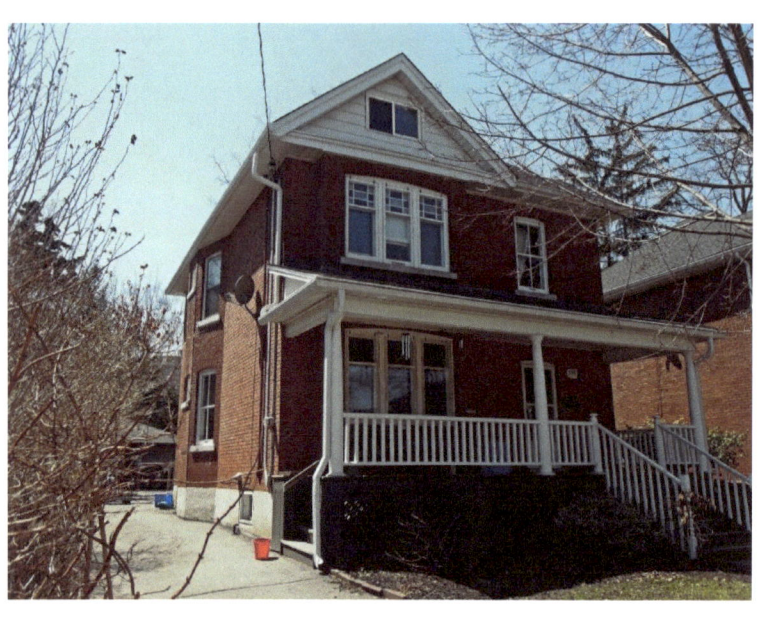

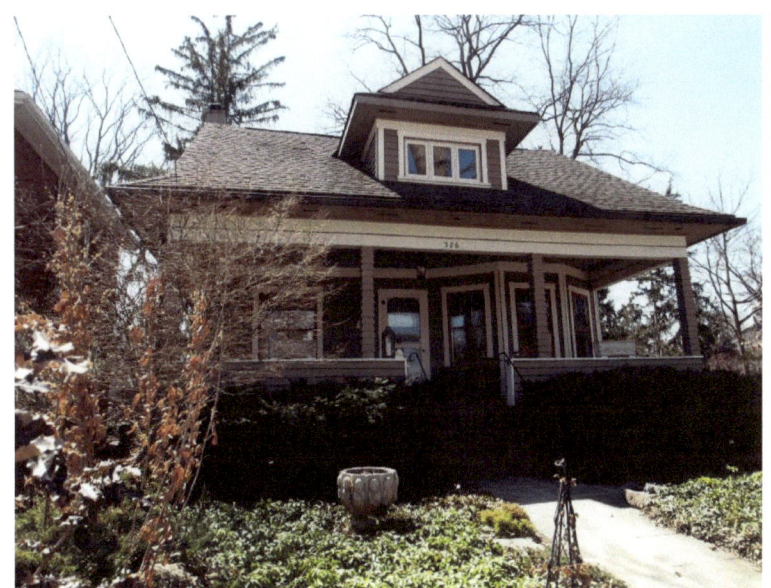

526 Burlington Avenue – Italianate – hipped roof, dormer

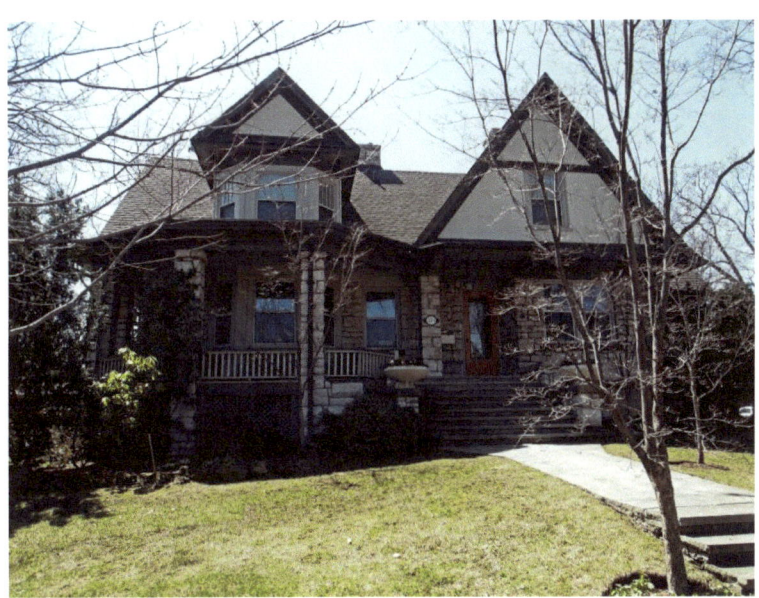

534 Burlington Avenue – Gothic Revival

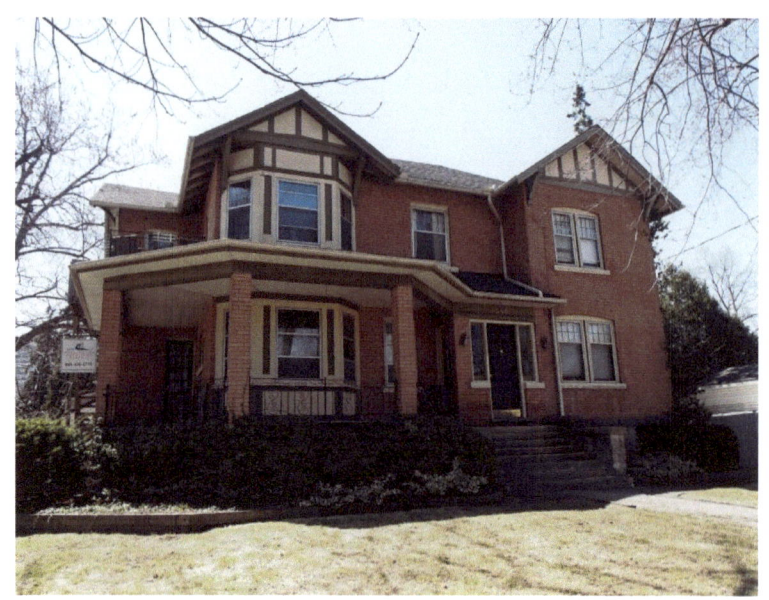

546 Burlington Avenue – Tudor accents

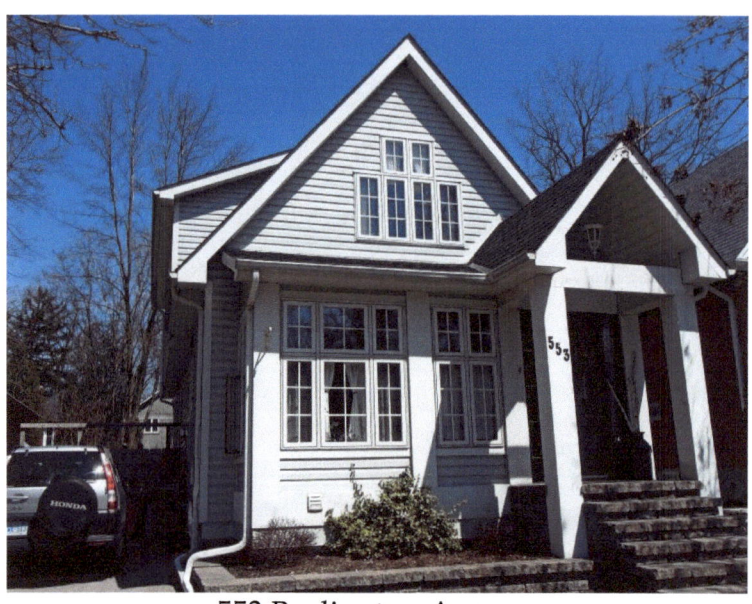

553 Burlington Avenue

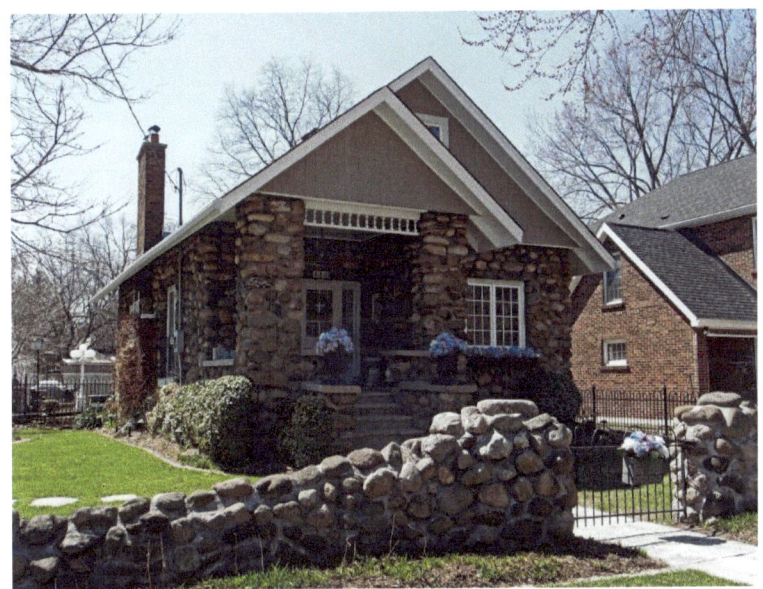

558 Burlington Avenue – cobblestone architecture

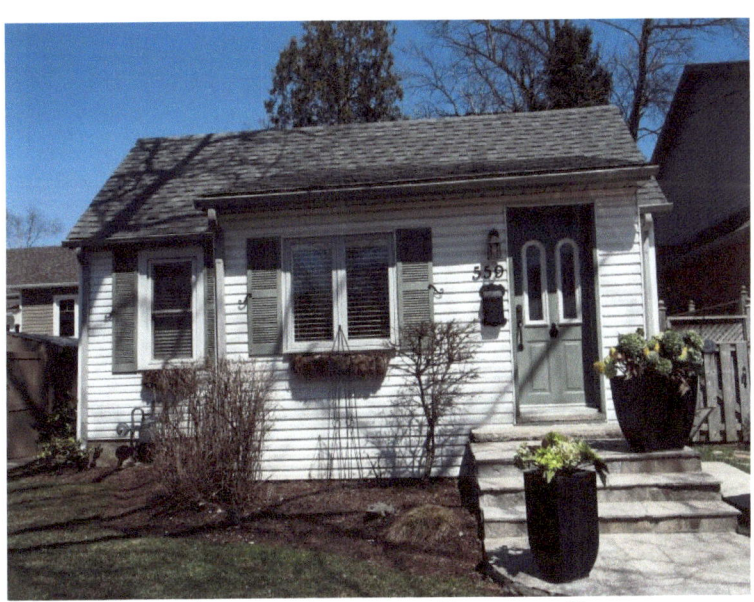

559 Burlington Avenue – Regency Cottage

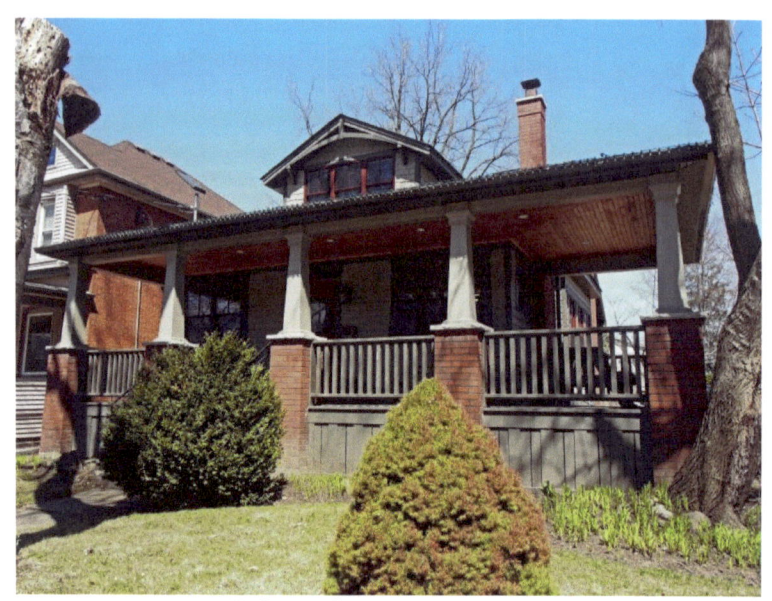

543 Burlington Avenue

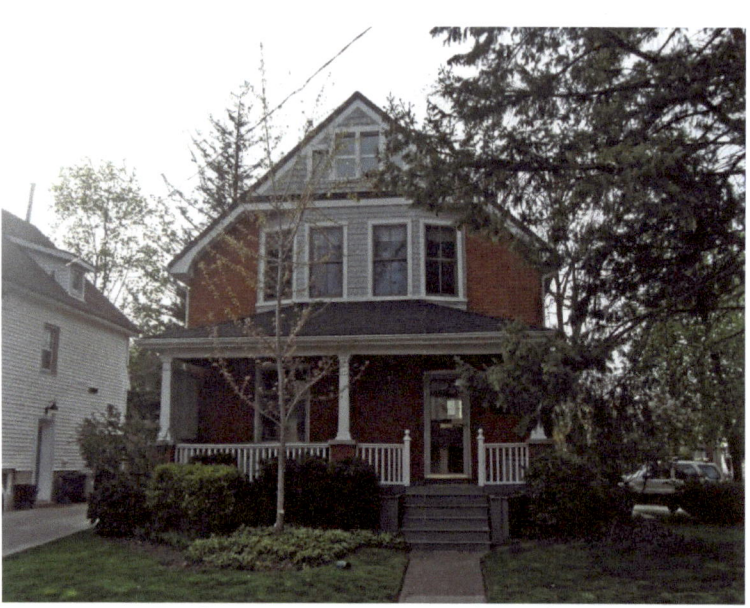

Burlington Avenue - Edwardian

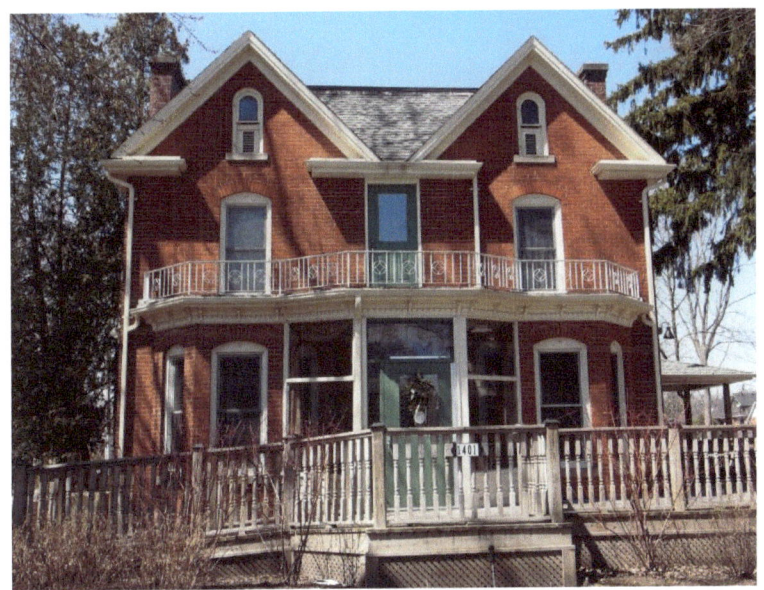

1401 Ontario Street – Gothic Revival – cornice return on gables, full verandah on second floor

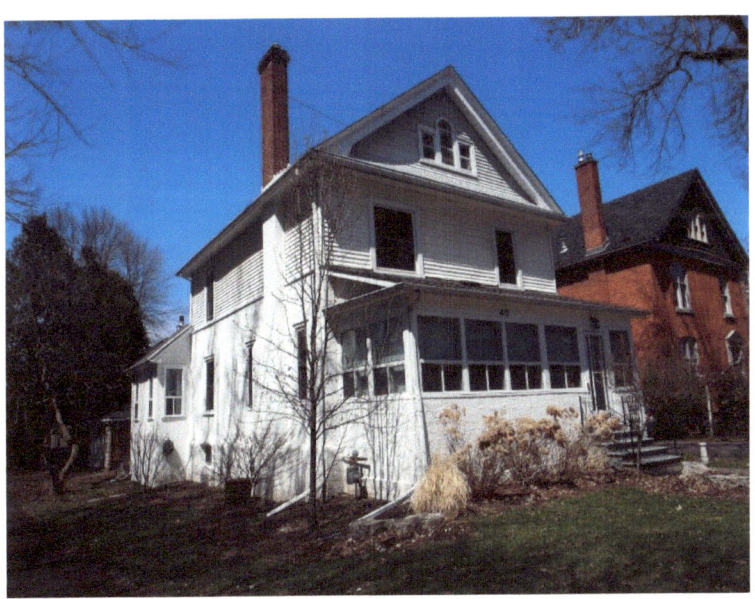

1413 Ontario Street – Edwardian, Palladian window in gable

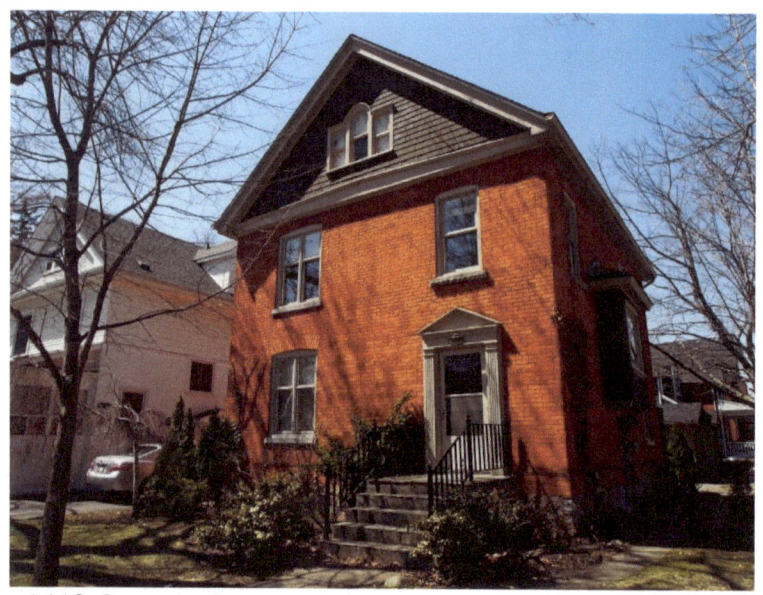

1419 Ontario Street – Edwardian, Palladian window

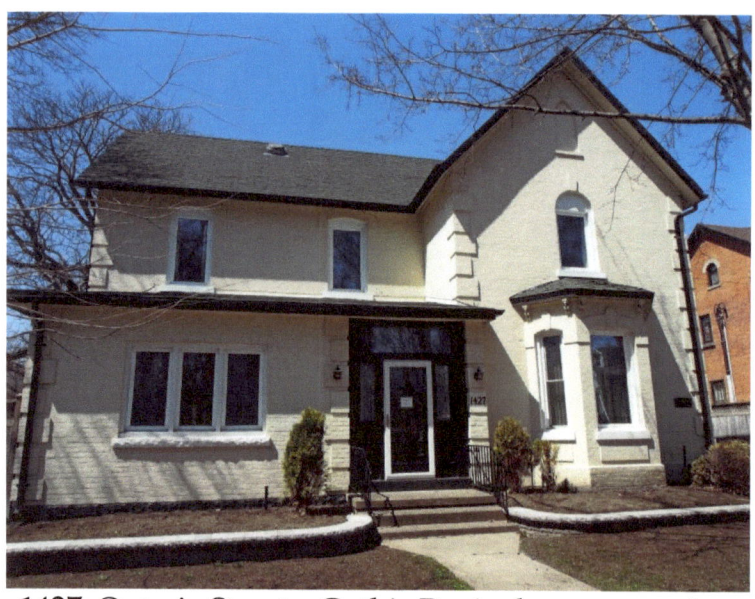

1427 Ontario Street – Gothic Revival, corner quoins, bay window with cornice brackets

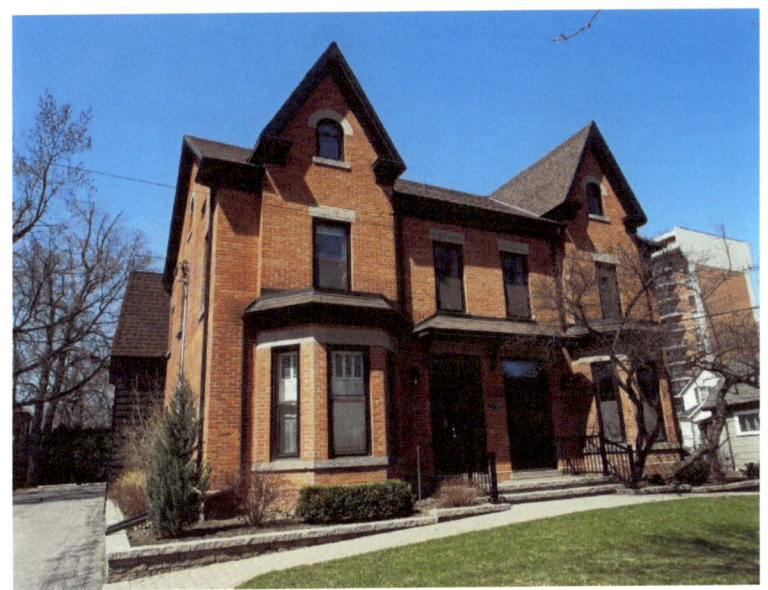

1433 Ontario Street – Gothic Revival,
bay windows on ground floor, cornice return on gables

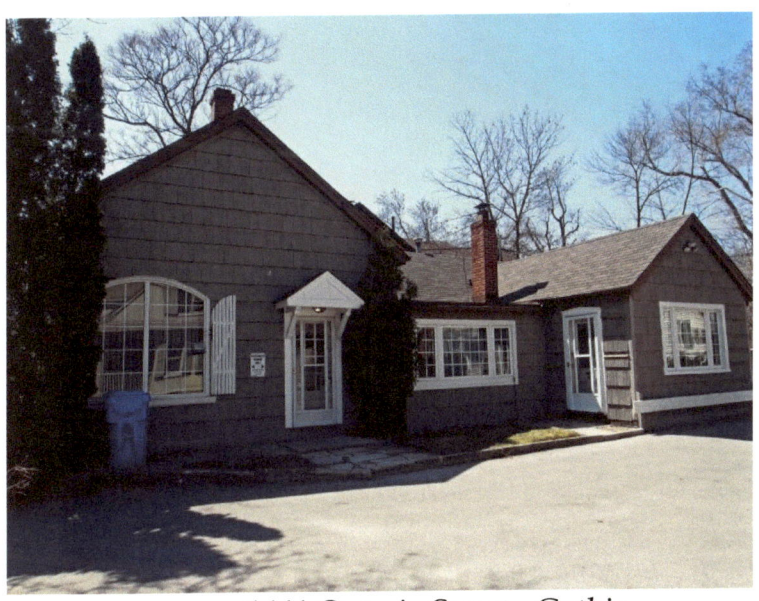

1441 Ontario Street - Gothic

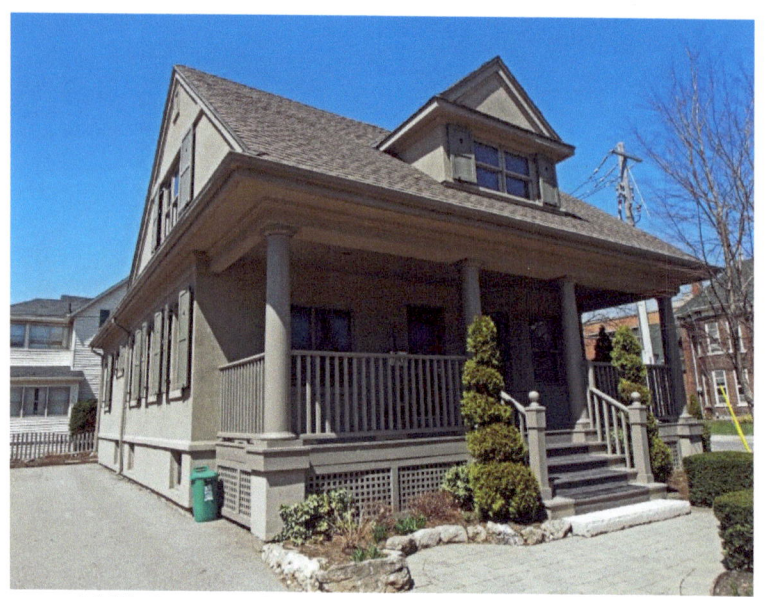

1445 Ontario Street – Gothic Revival, dormer

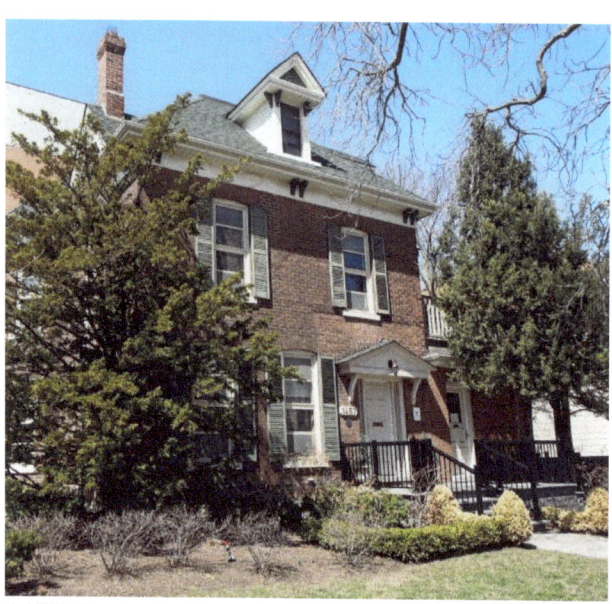

1457 Ontario Street – Italianate, hipped roof, dormer in attic

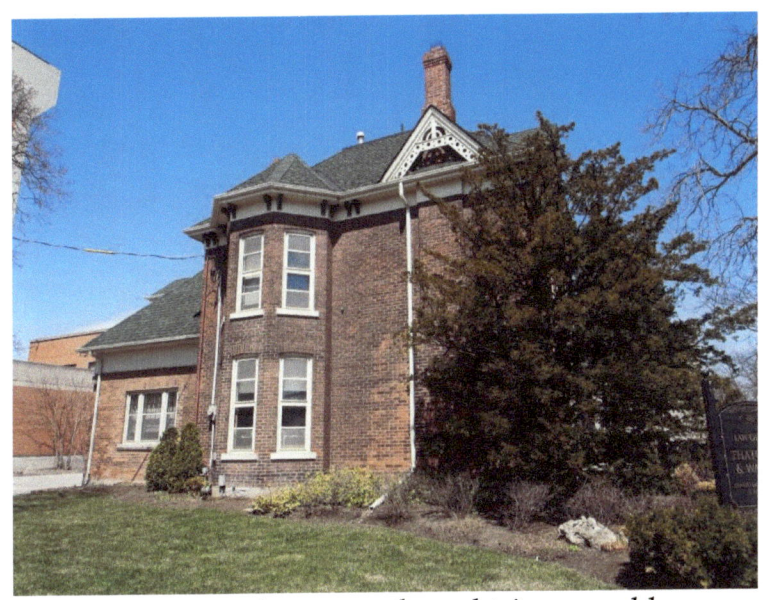

Two-storey bay, vergeboard trim on gable,
paired cornice brackets

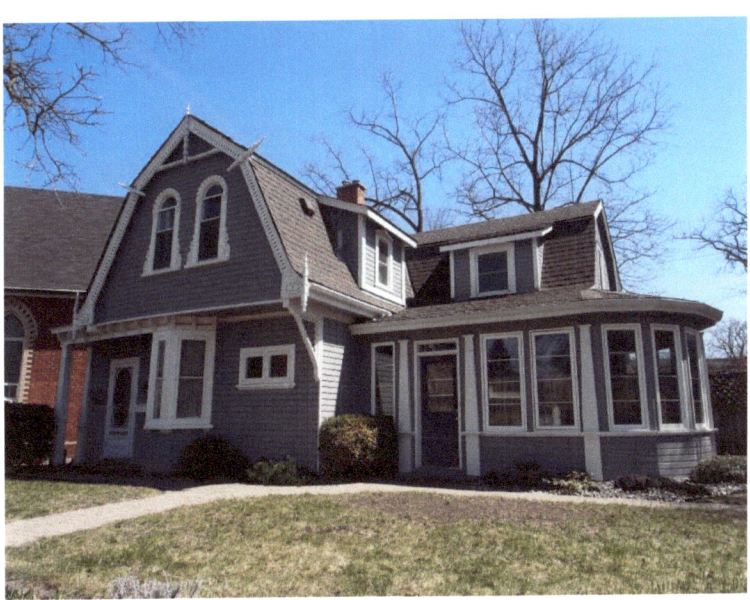

1442 Ontario Street – The Manse

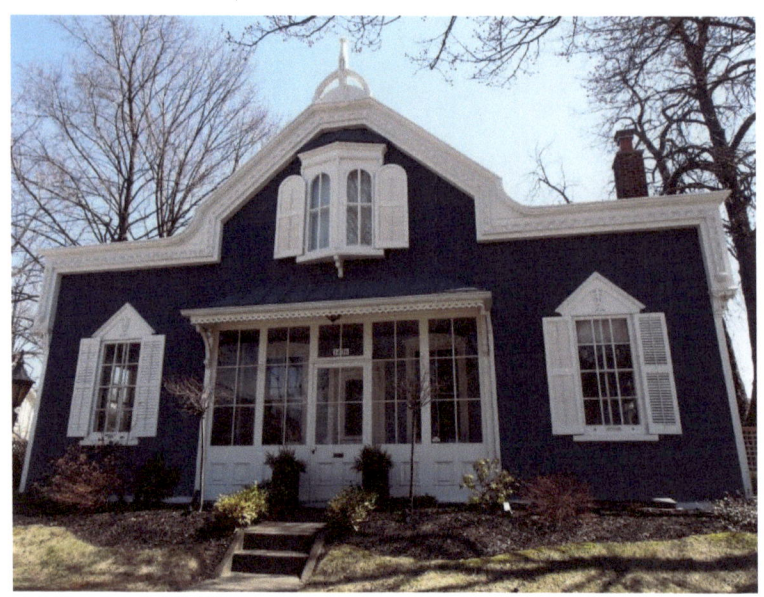

1436 Ontario Street – finial on gable

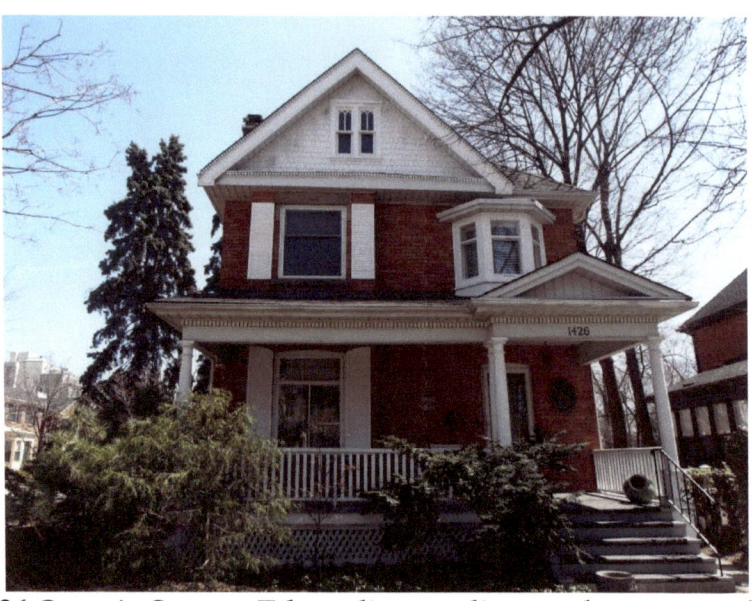

1426 Ontario Street – Edwardian, pediment above verandah

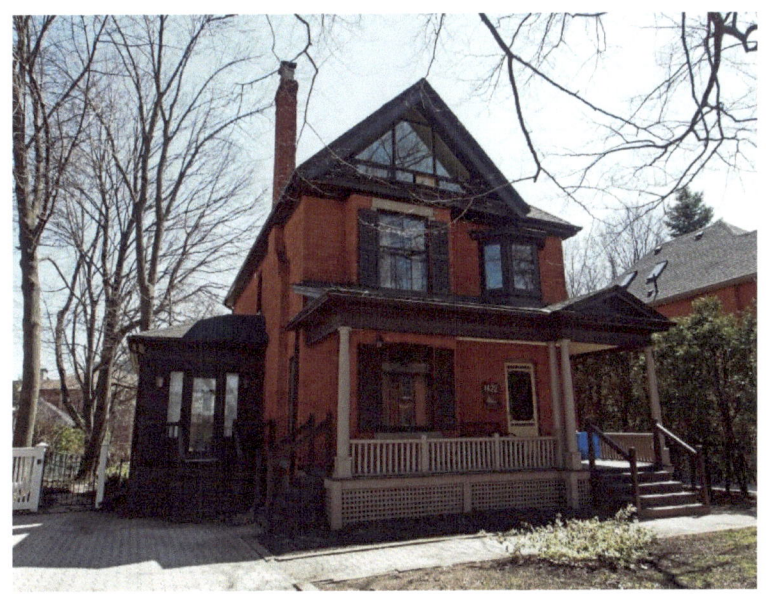

1422 Ontario Street – Edwardian, pediment

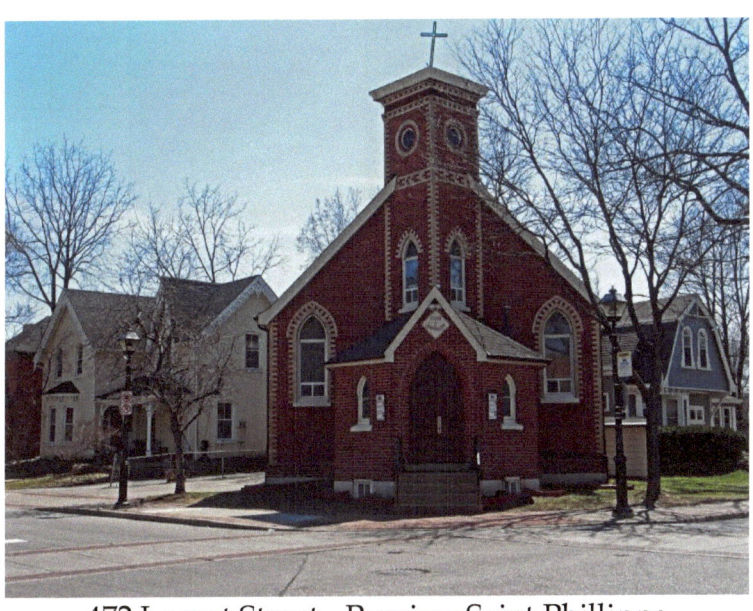

472 Locust Street - Paroisse Saint Phillippe

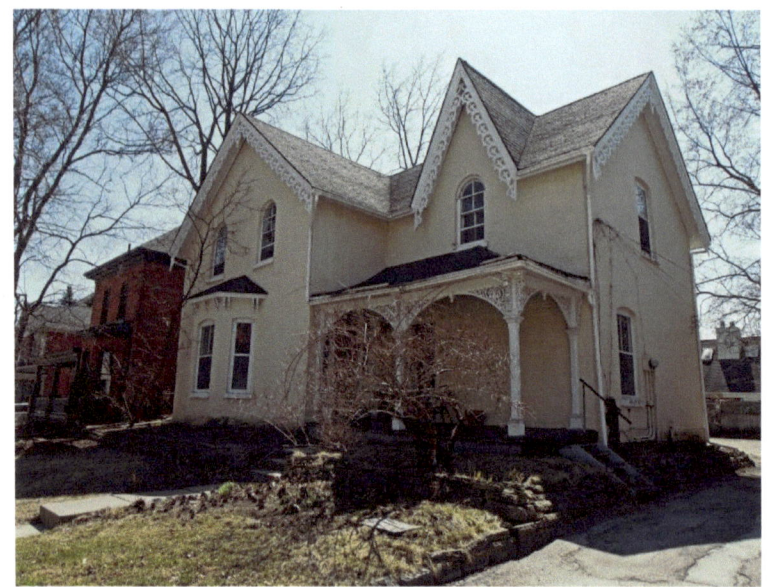

468 Locust Street – Gothic Revival – vergeboard trim on gables, bay window

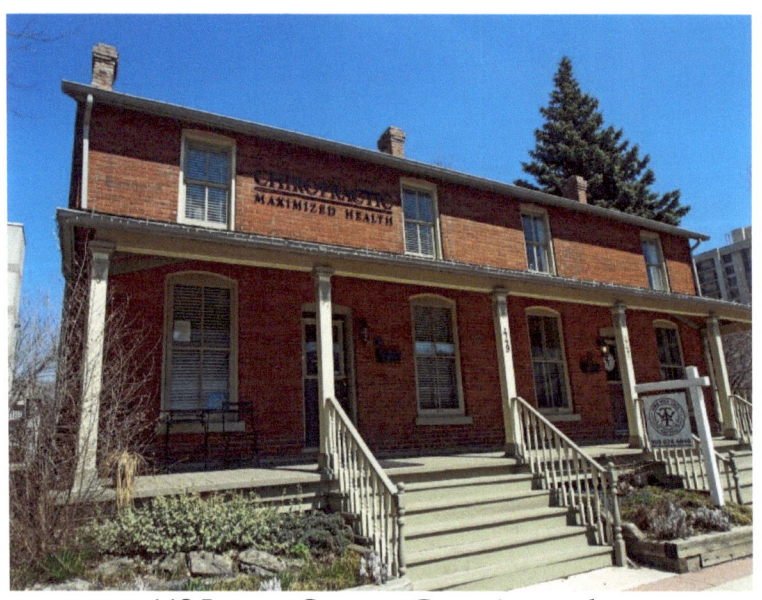

449 Locust Street – Georgian style

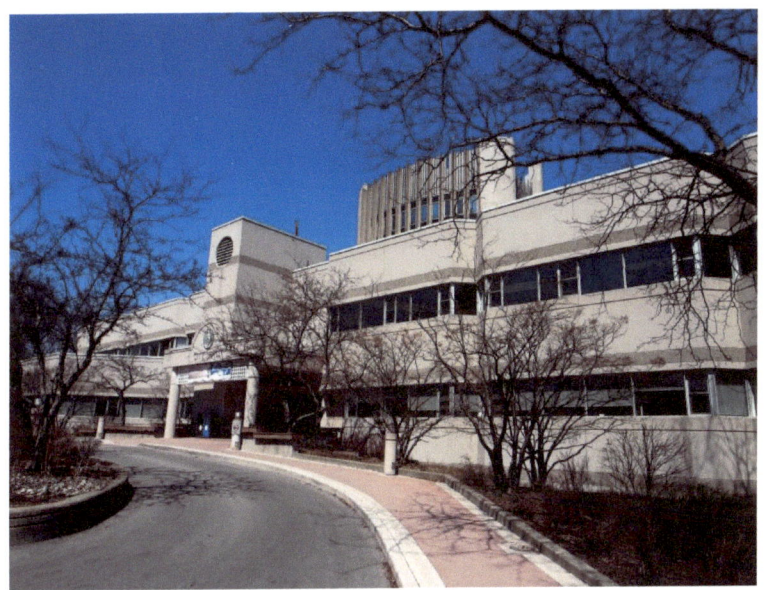

Burlington City Hall

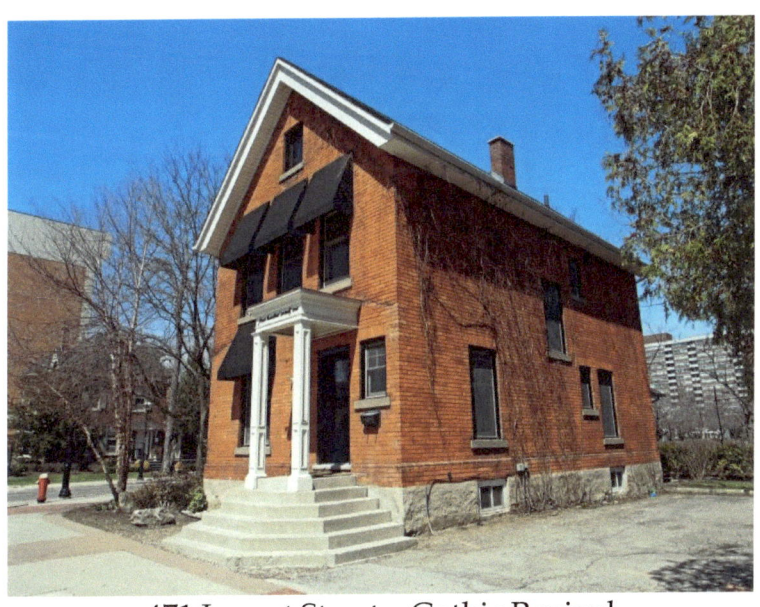

471 Locust Street – Gothic Revival

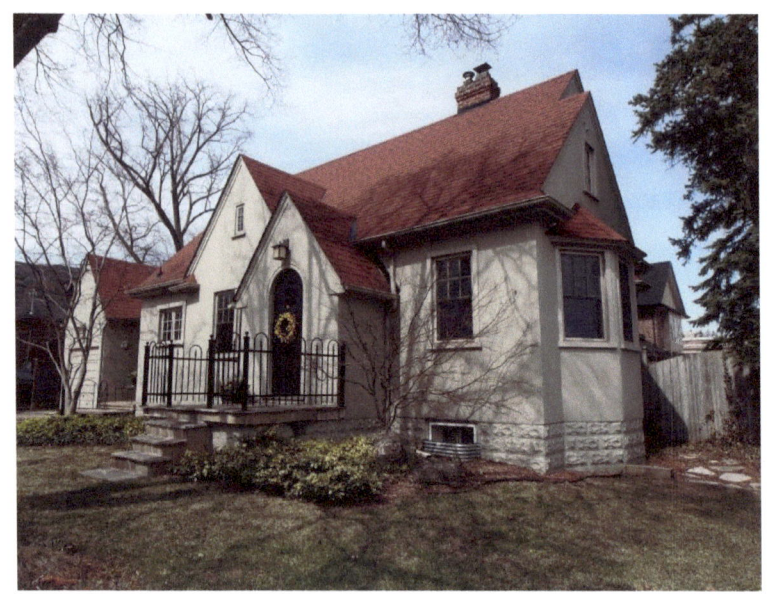

535 Locust Street – Gothic Revival

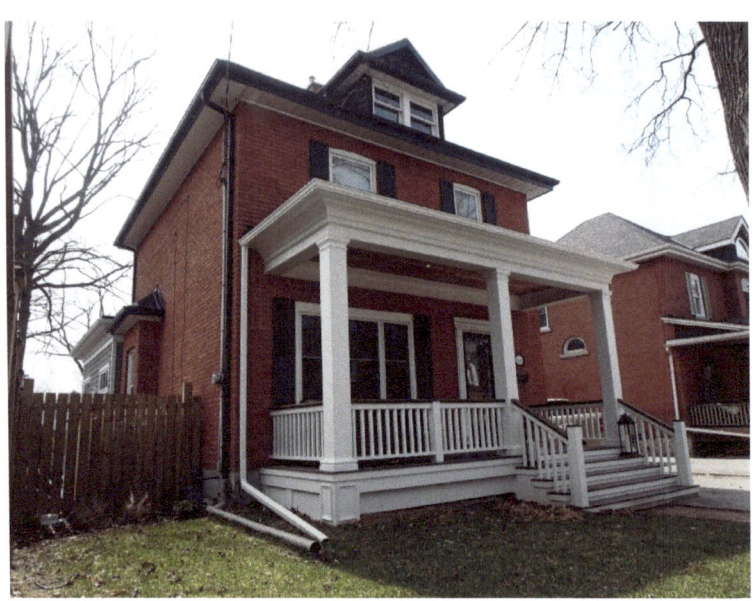

540 Locust Street – Italianate - dormer

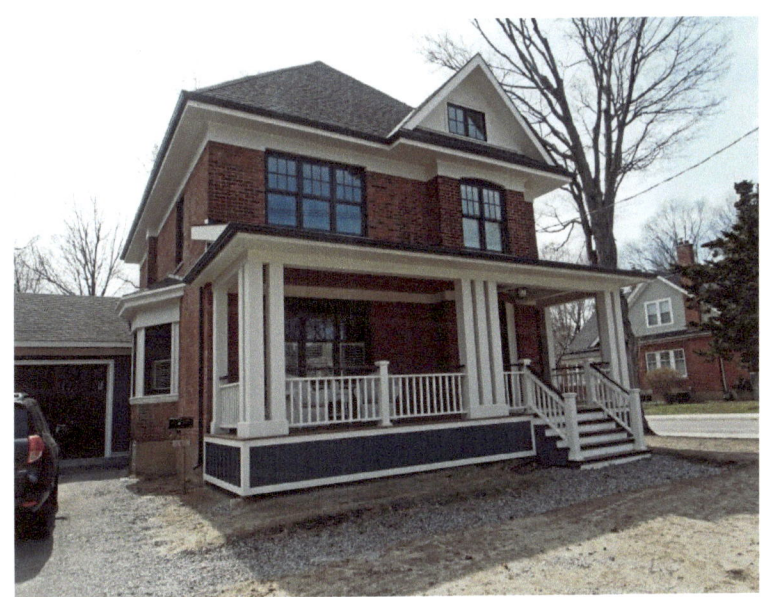

Locust Street – Italianate – hipped roof

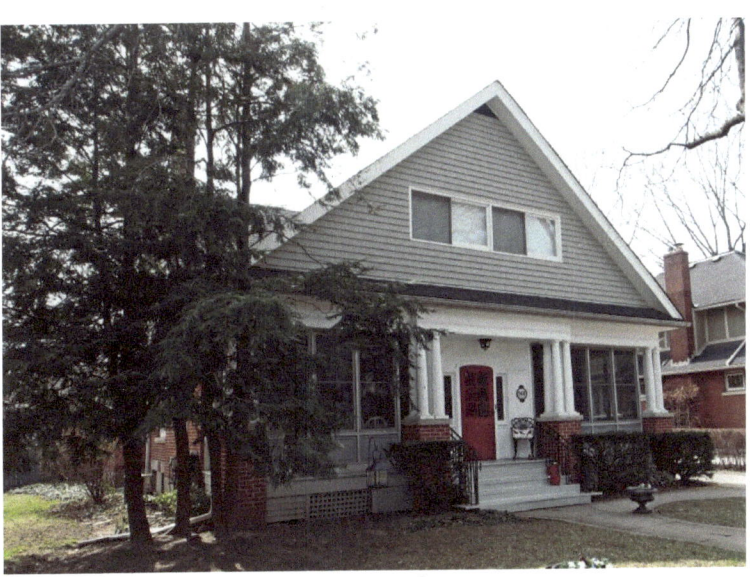

560 Locust Street

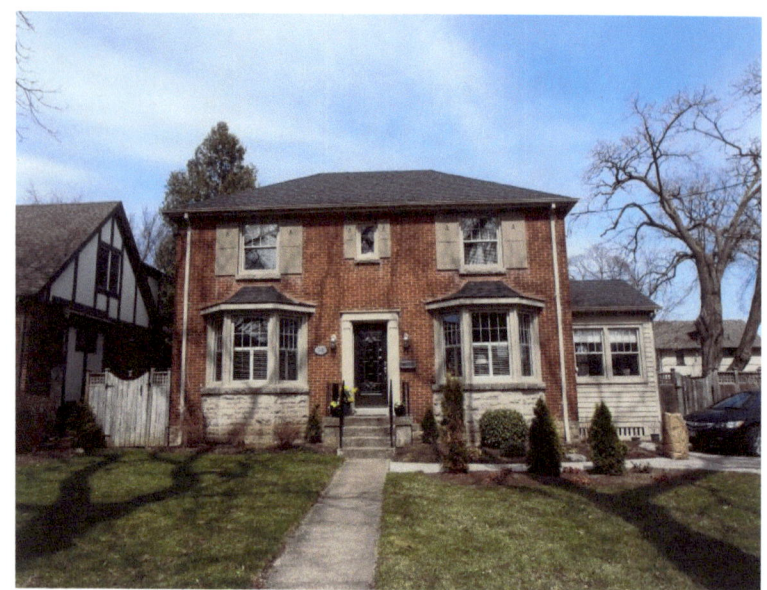

561 Locust Street – Italianate – hipped roof, bay windows

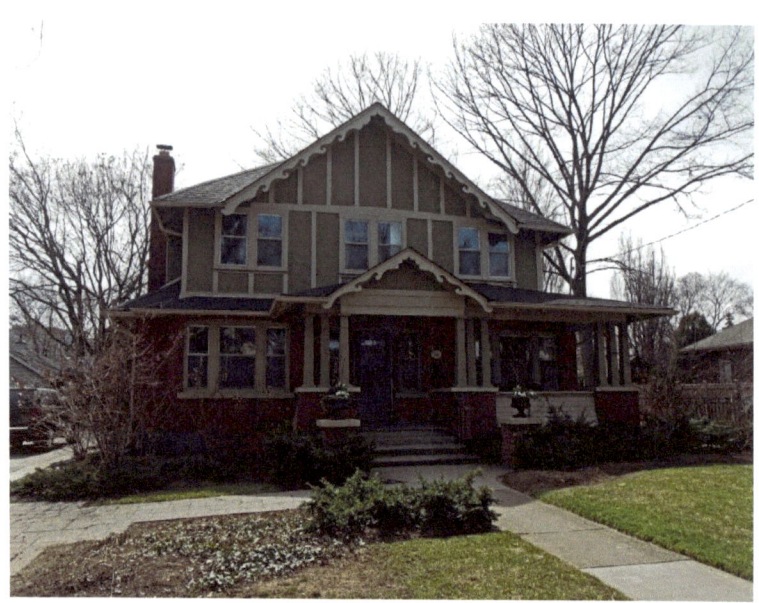

566 Locust Street – Tudor style, vergeboard trim

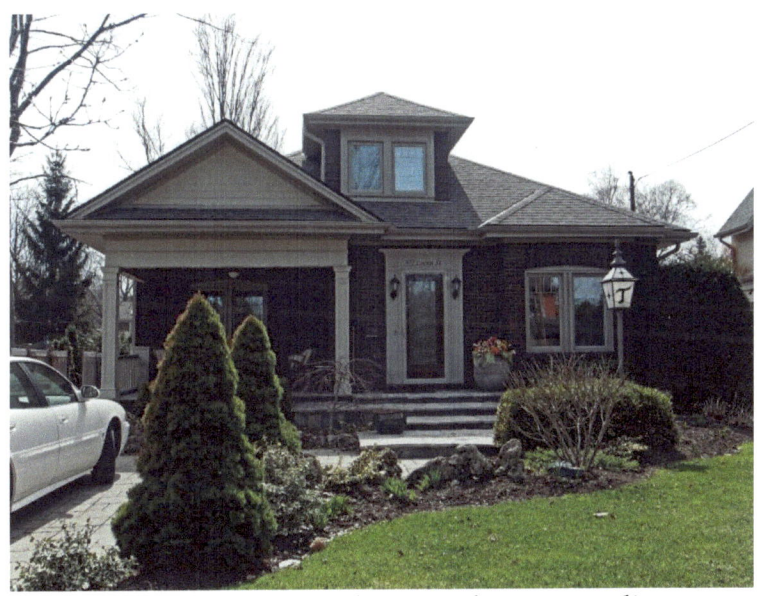

572 Locust Street – Italianate, dormer, pediment

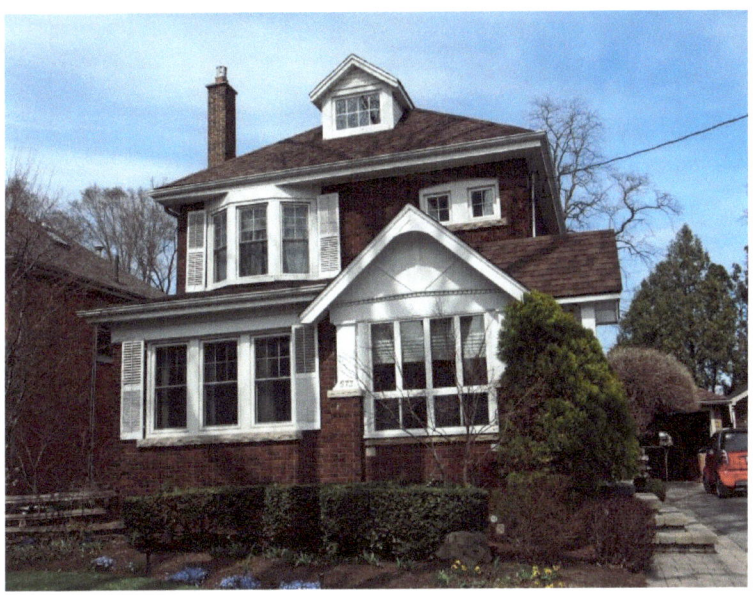

Locust Street – Italianate, dormer in attic

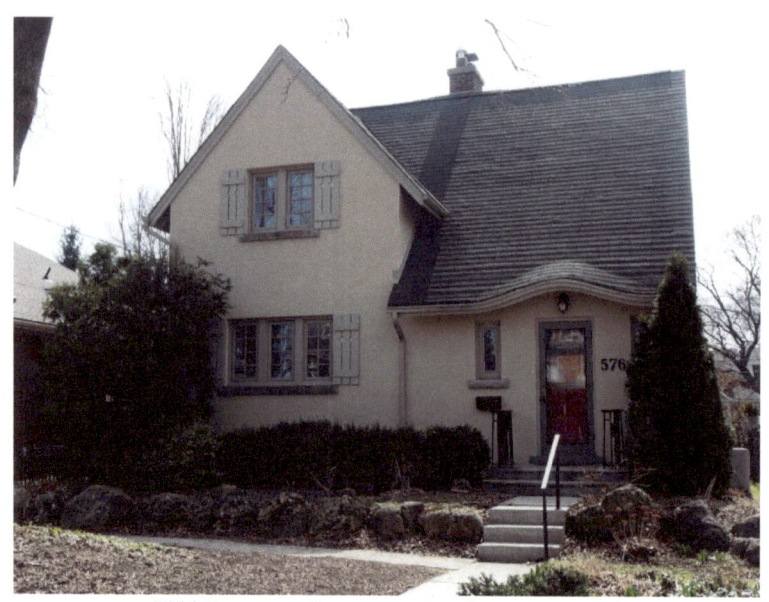

576 Locust Street – Gothic Revival

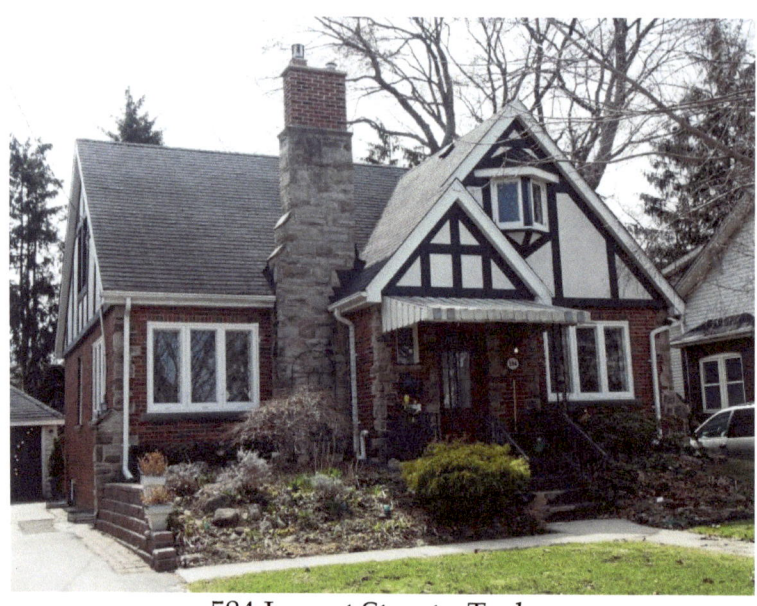

584 Locust Street - Tudor

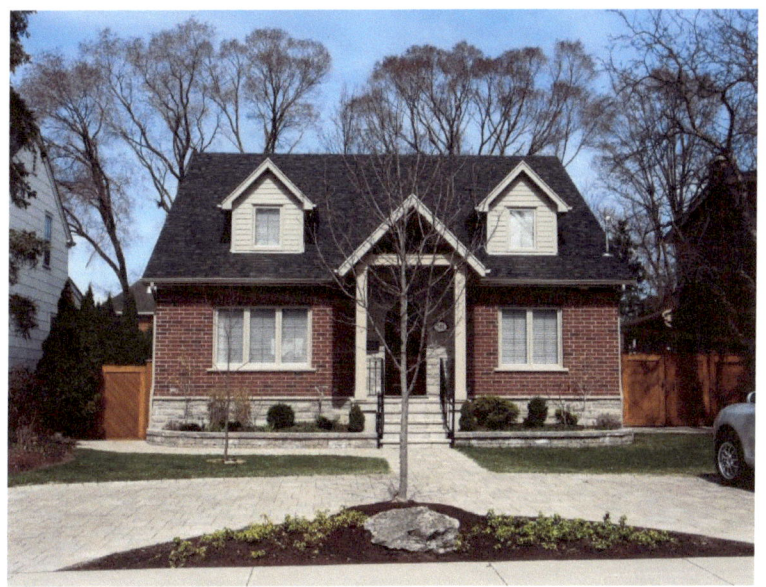

585 Locust Street - dormers

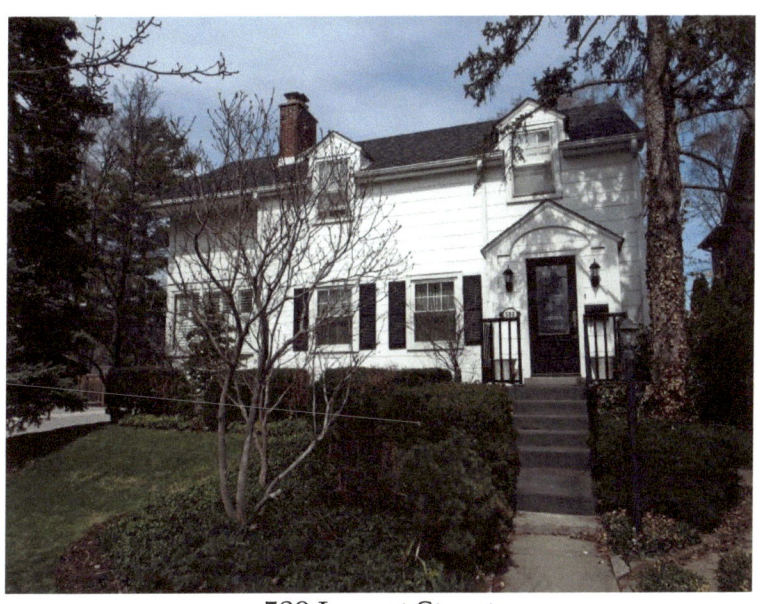

589 Locust Street

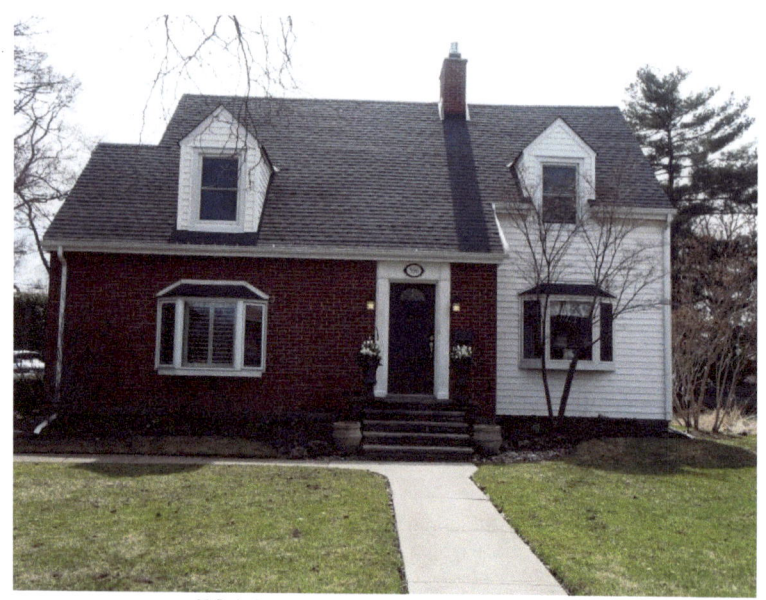

596 Locust Street - dormers

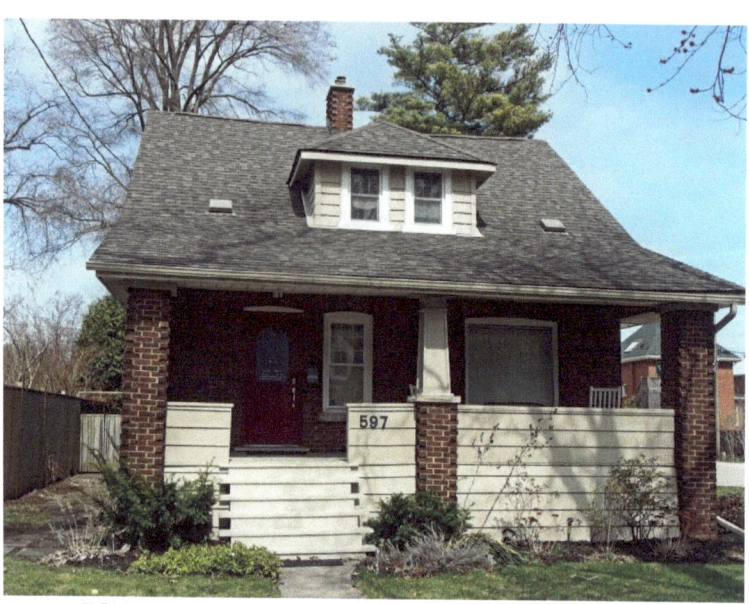

597 Locust Street –dormer above verandah

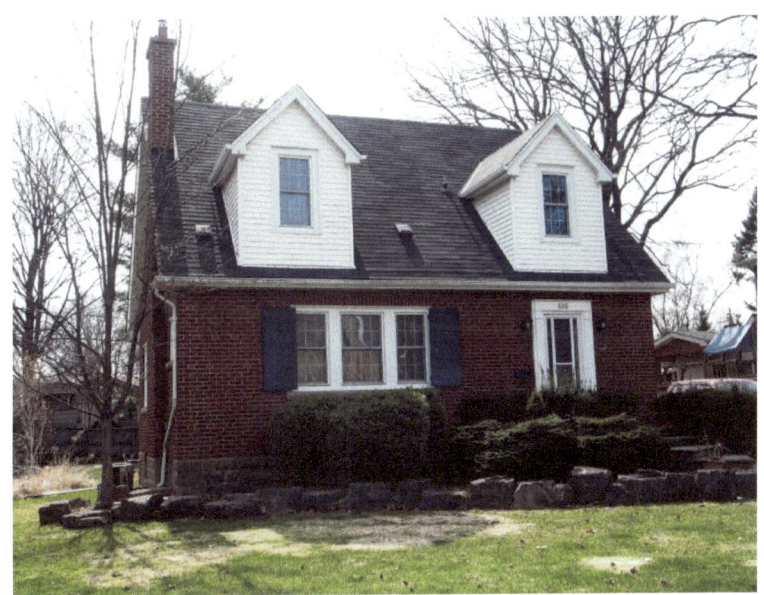

606 Locust Street - dormers

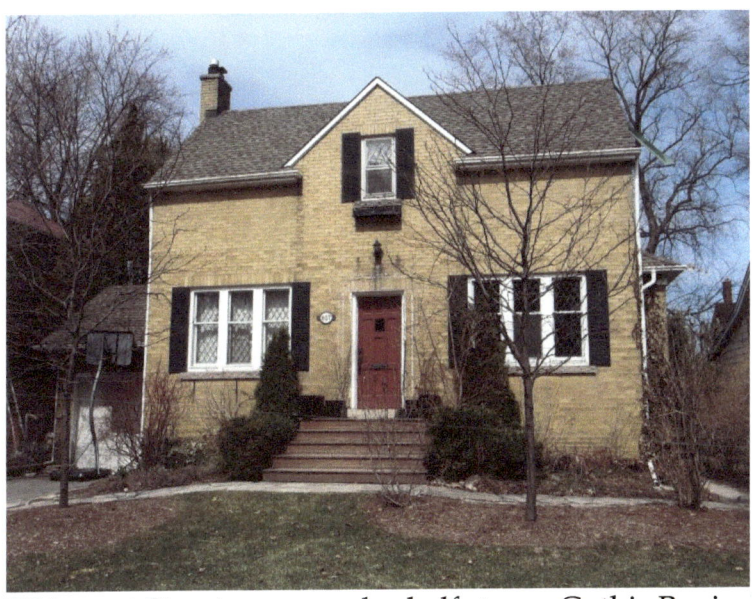

607 Locust Street – one-and-a-half storey Gothic Revival

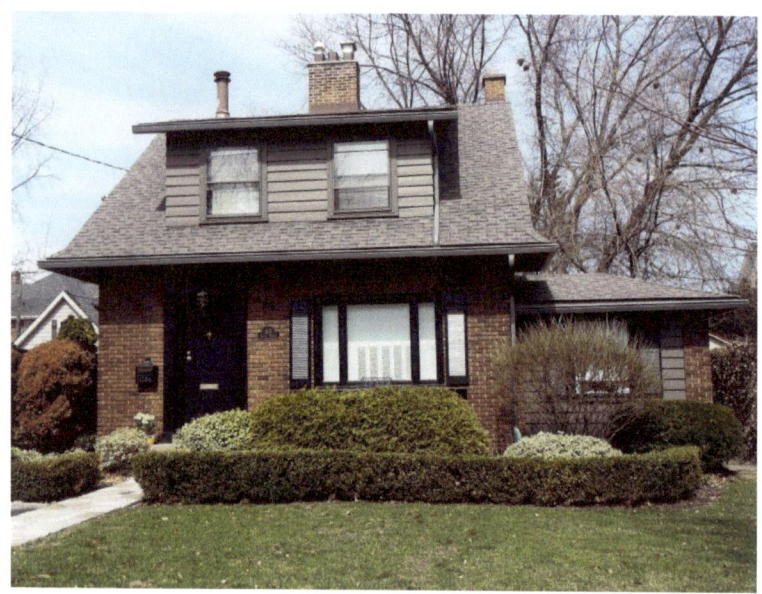

615 Locust Street

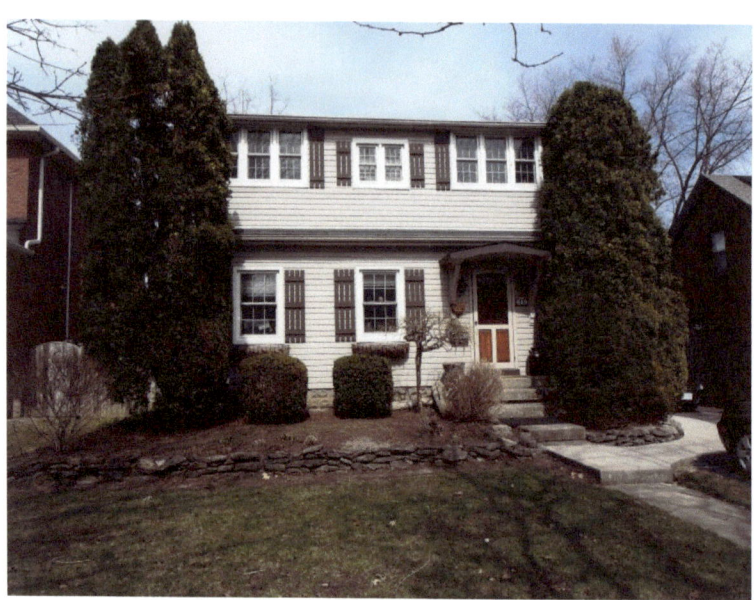

619 Locust Street - Georgian

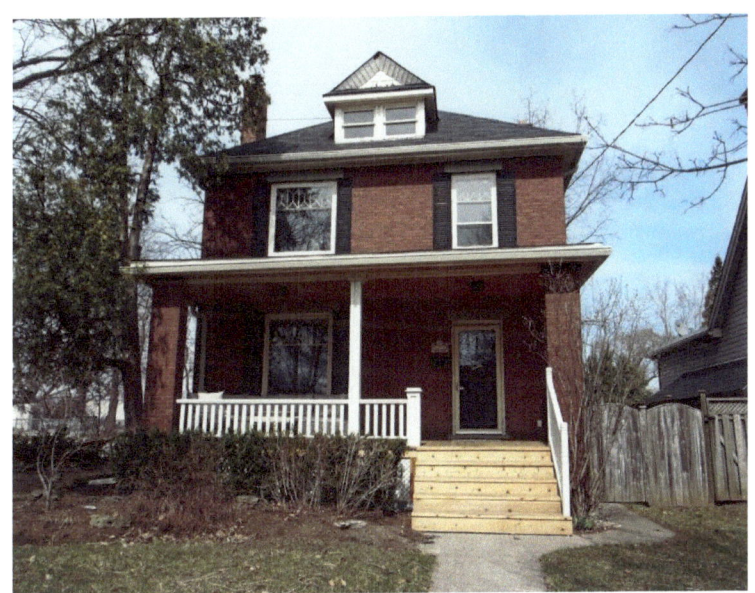

623 Locust Street – Italianate –dormer in attic

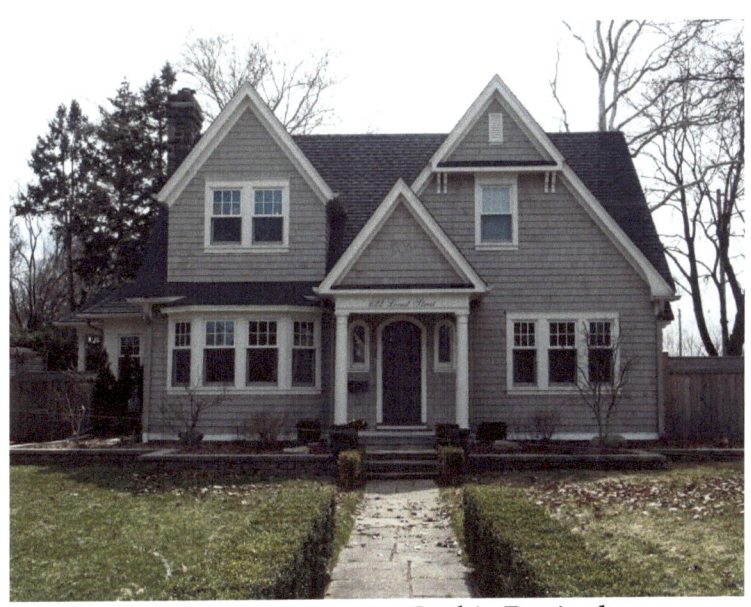

622 Locust Street – Gothic Revival

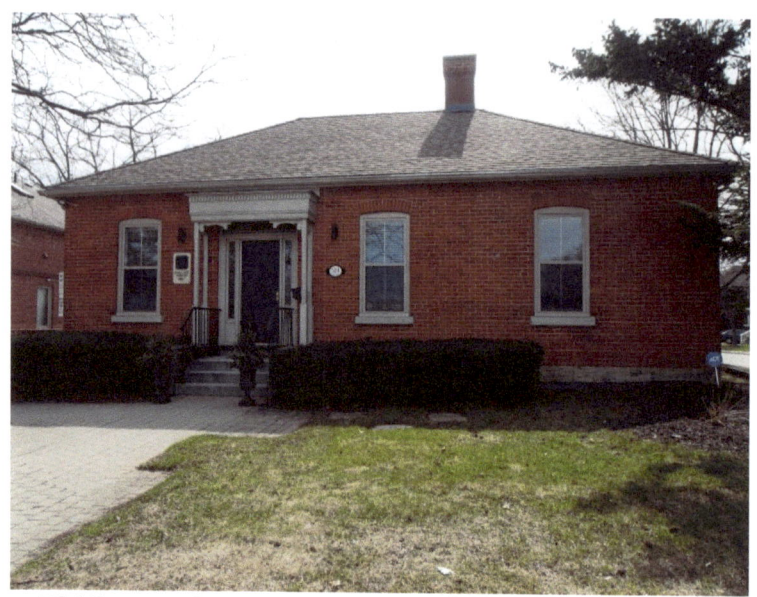

524 Locust Street – Regency Cottage – hipped roof

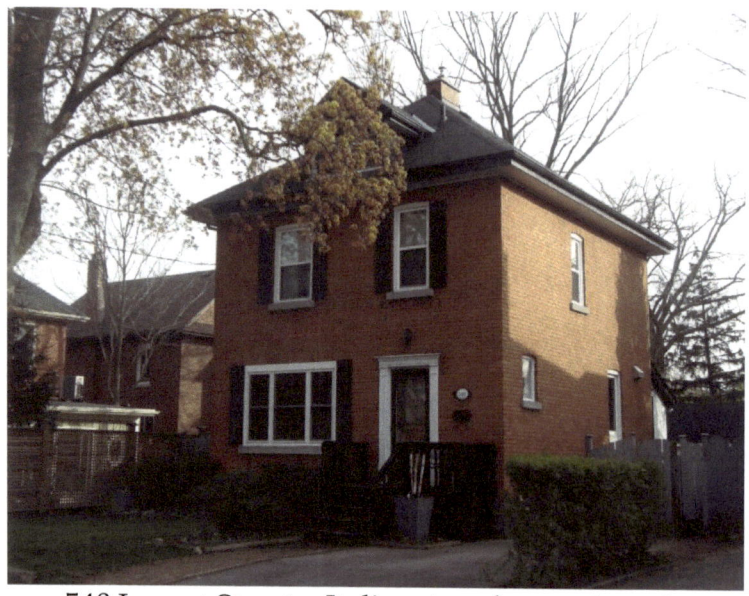

540 Locust Street – Italianate – dormer in attic

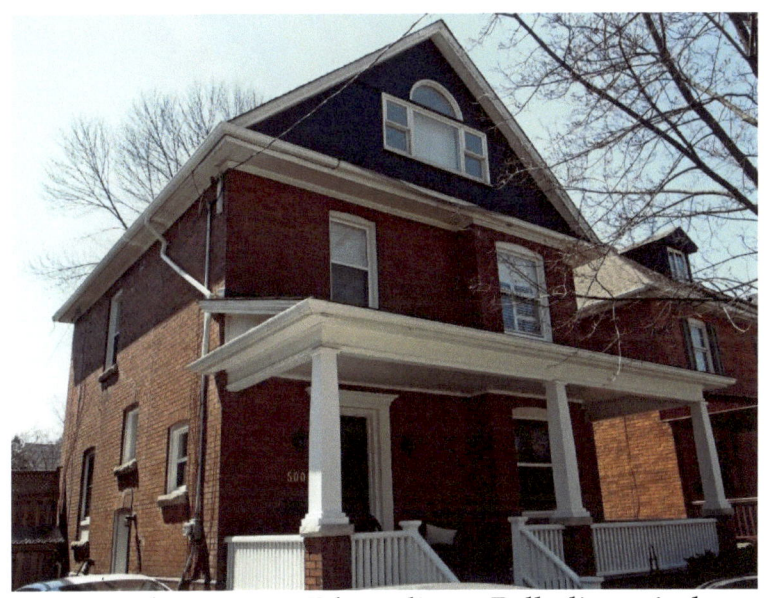

500 Hurd Avenue – Edwardian – Palladian window

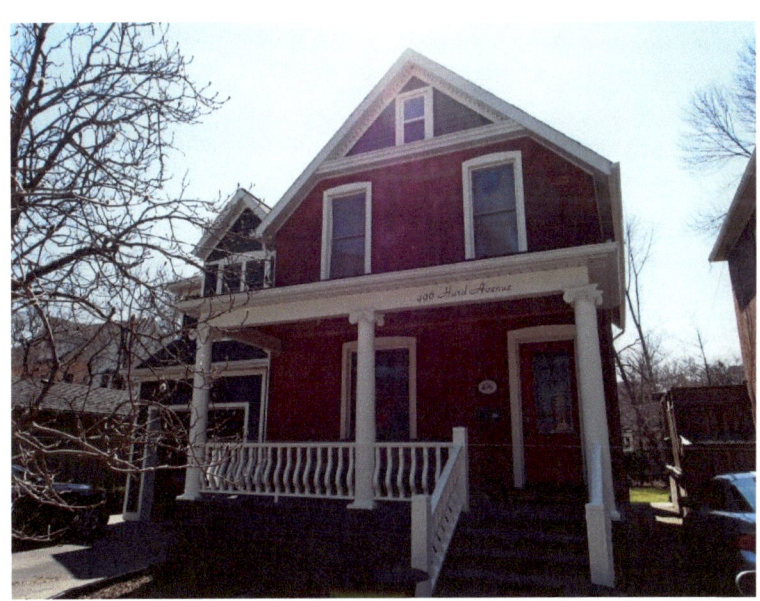

496 Hurd Avenue -Edwardian

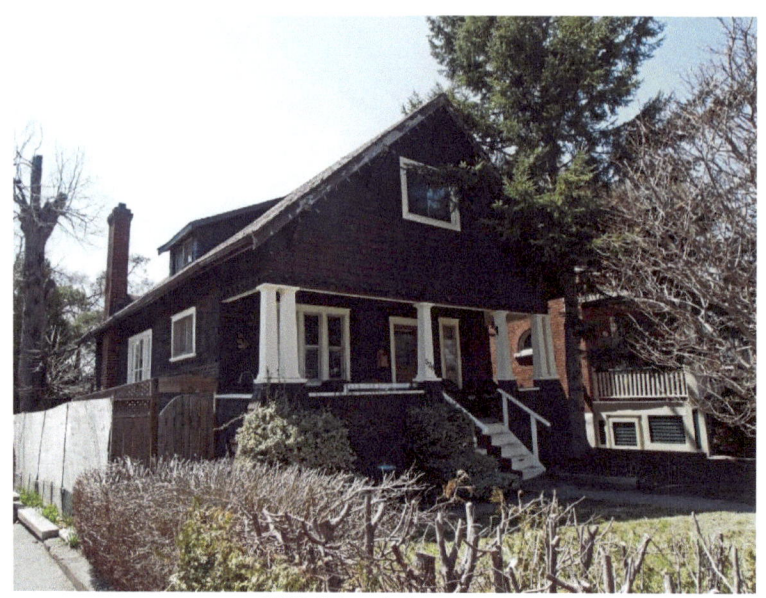

528 Hurd Avenue

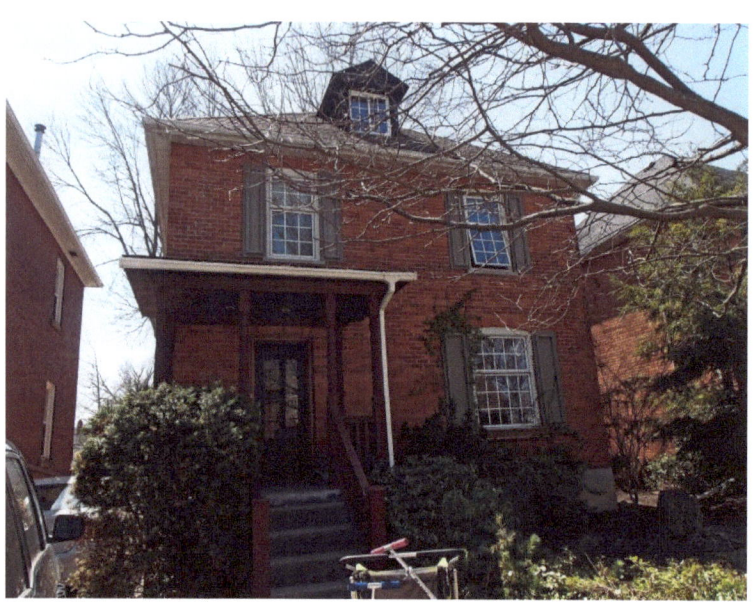

504 Hurd Avenue – Italianate – dormer in attic

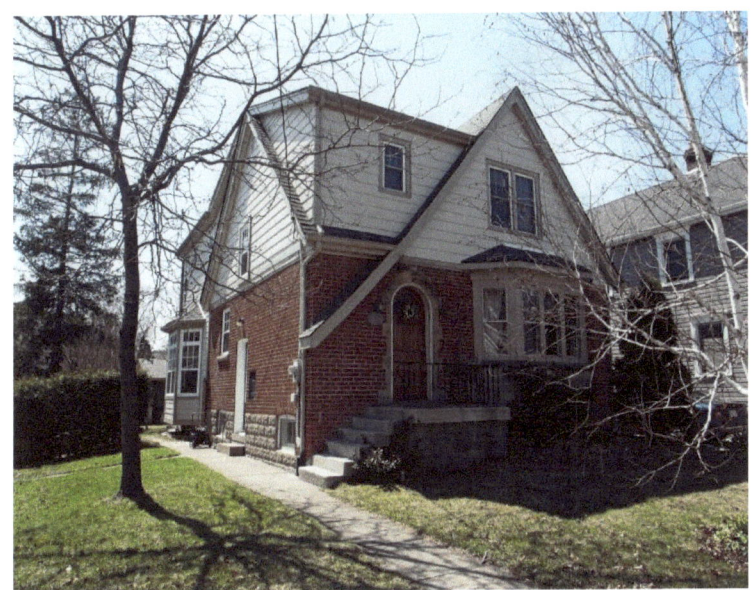

540 Hurd Avenue

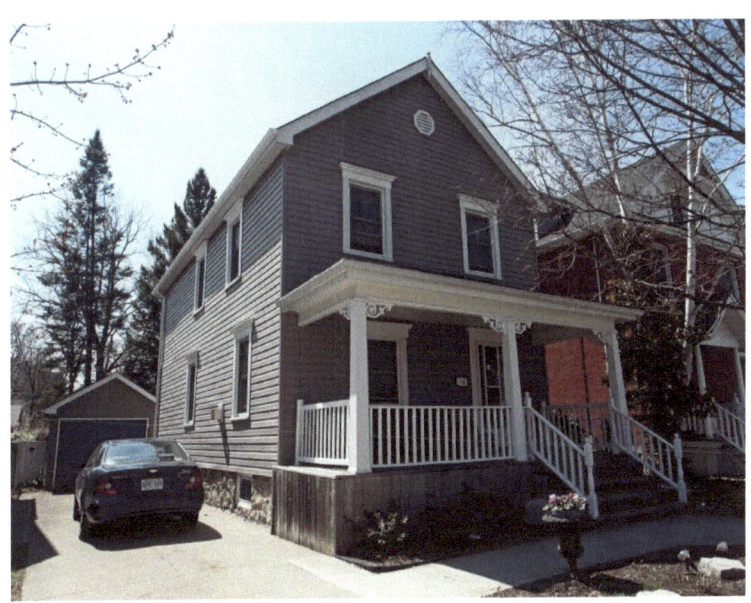

544 Hurd Avenue – Gothic Revival

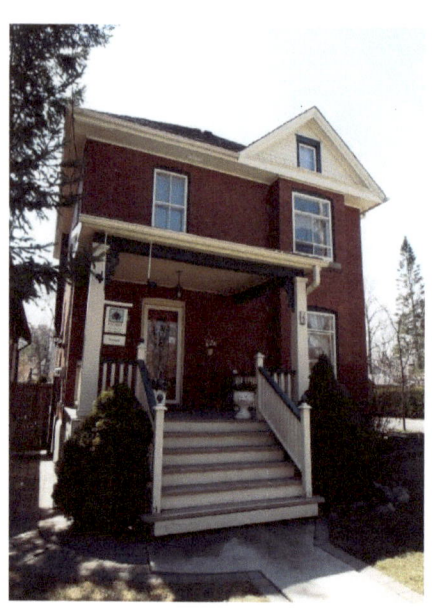

532 Hurd Avenue – Heart of Burlington Bed and Breakfast
Italianate with two-and-a-half storey tower-like bay with
gable, bay window on side

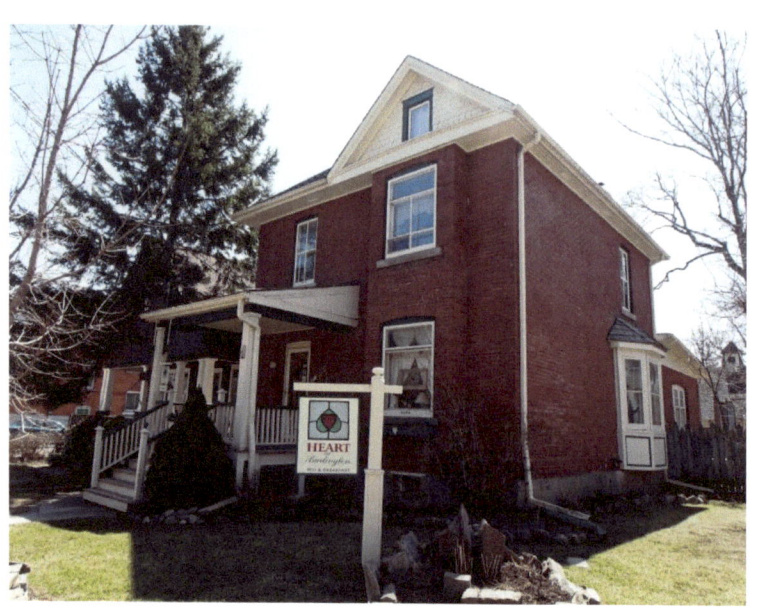

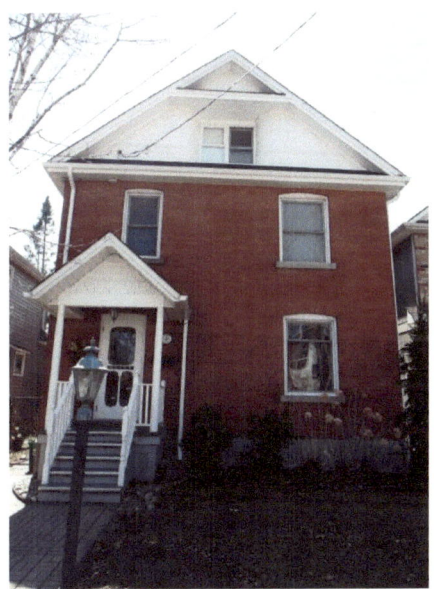

546 Hurd Avenue - Edwardian

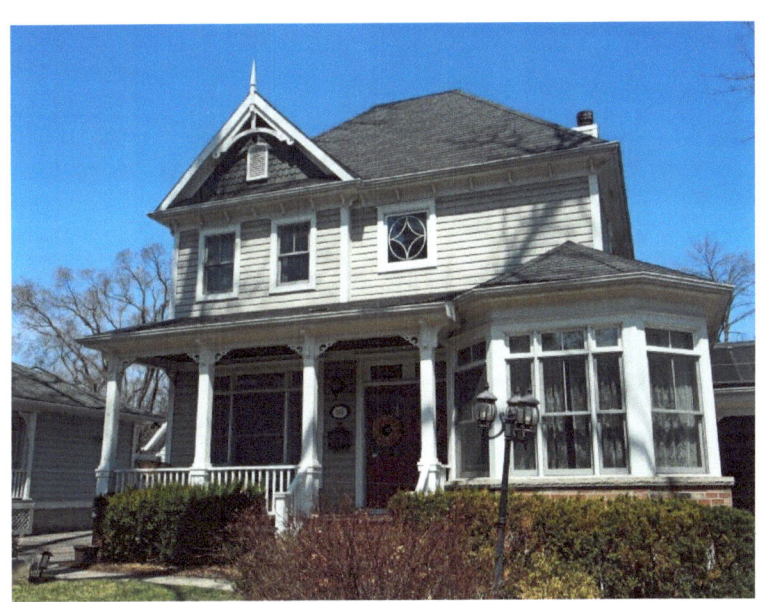

551 Hurd Avenue – Italianate – hipped roof, finial on gable

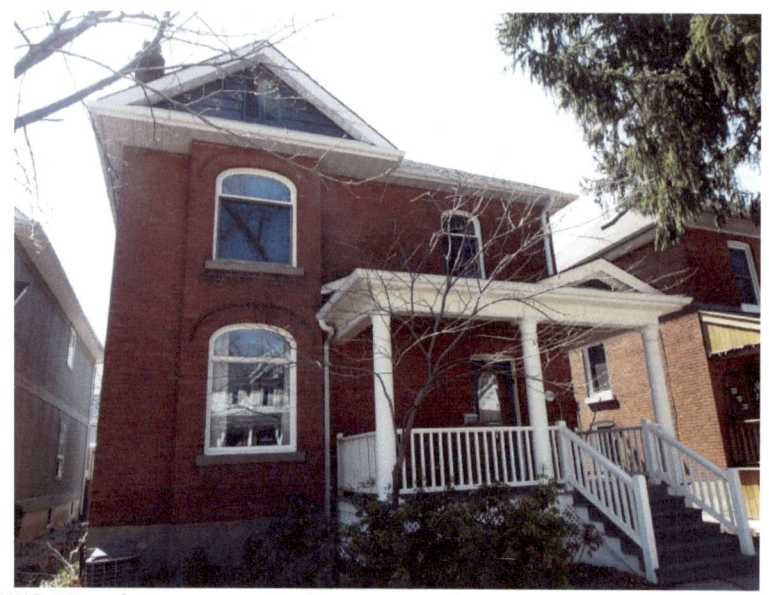

550 Hurd Avenue - Italianate with two-and-a-half storey tower-like bay with gable

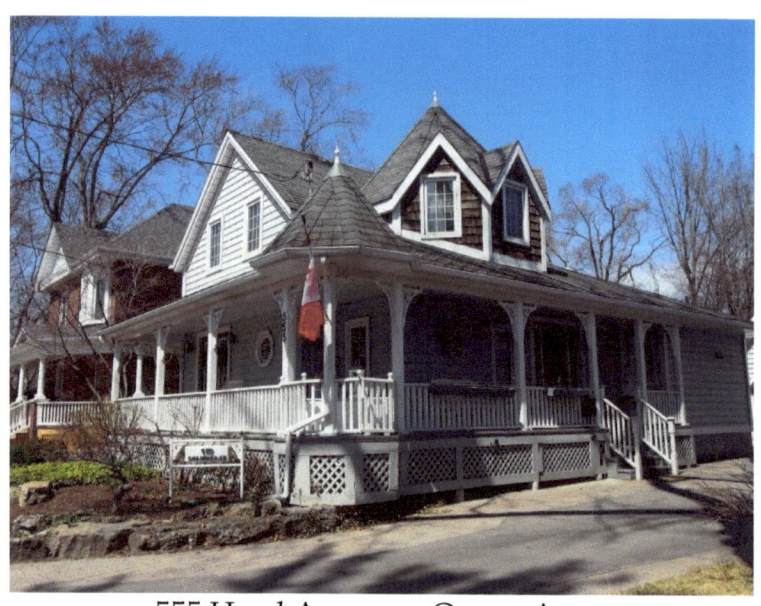

555 Hurd Avenue – Queen Anne

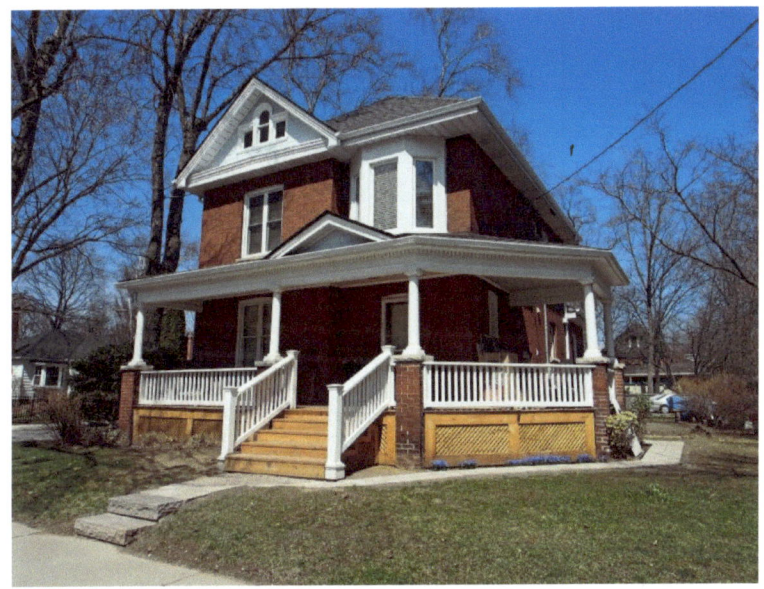

559 Hurd Avenue – Edwardian, Palladian window, second floor bay window, wrap-around verandah, pediment above door

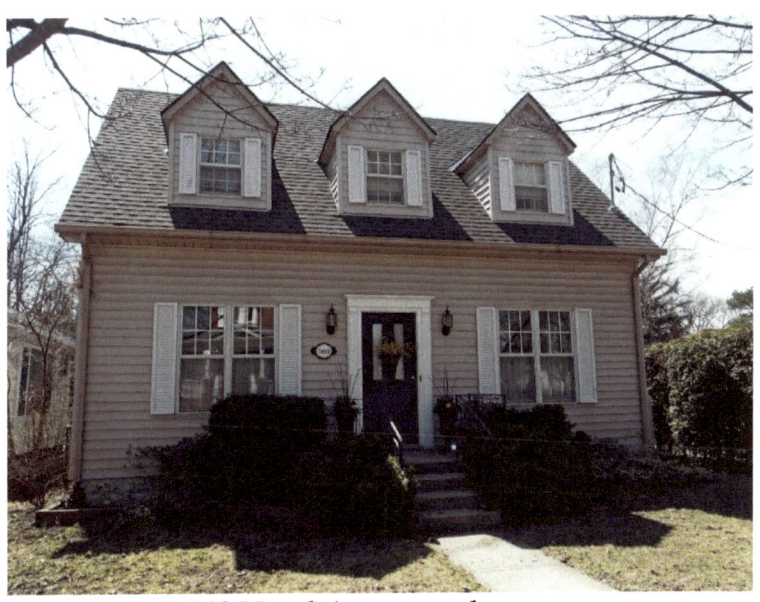

560 Hurd Avenue - dormers

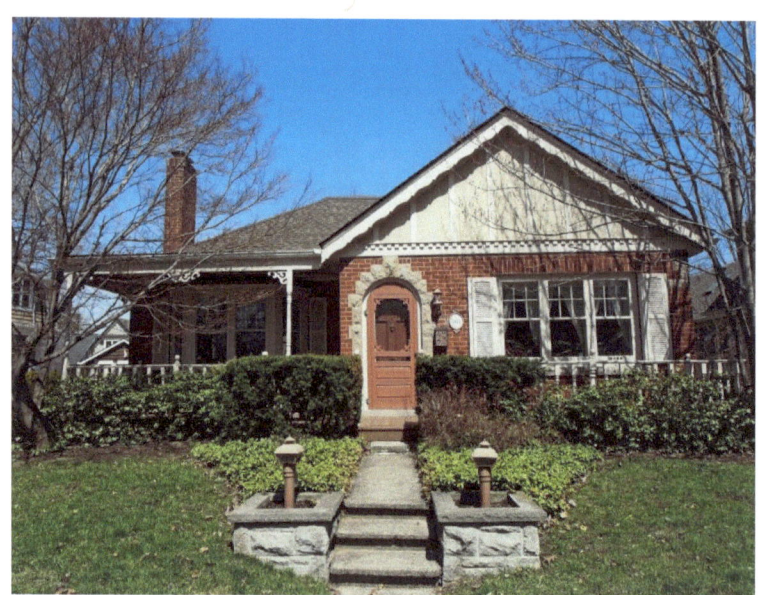

581 Hurd Avenue

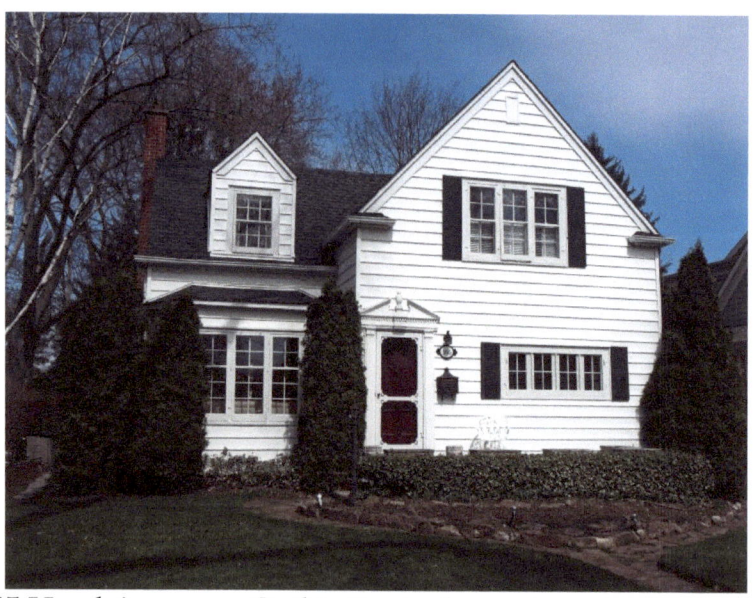

595 Hurd Avenue – Gothic Revival, cornice return, dormer

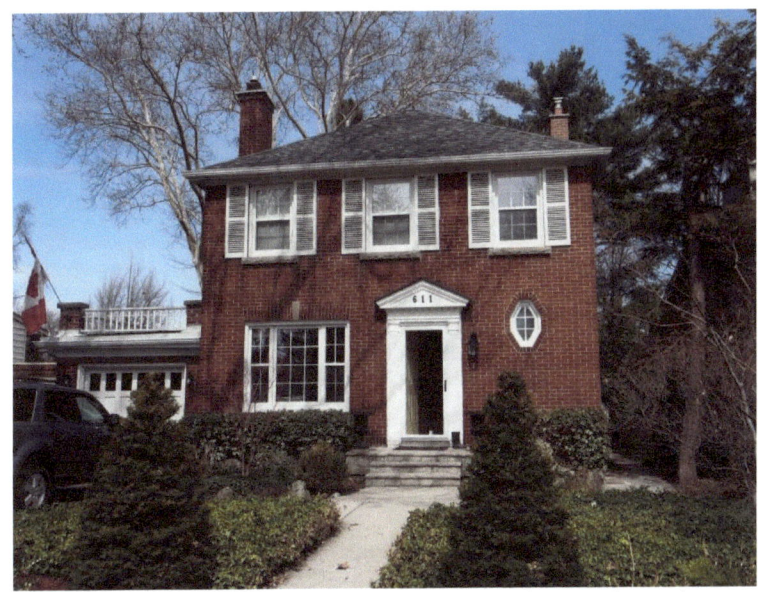

611 Hurd Avenue – Italianate – hipped roof

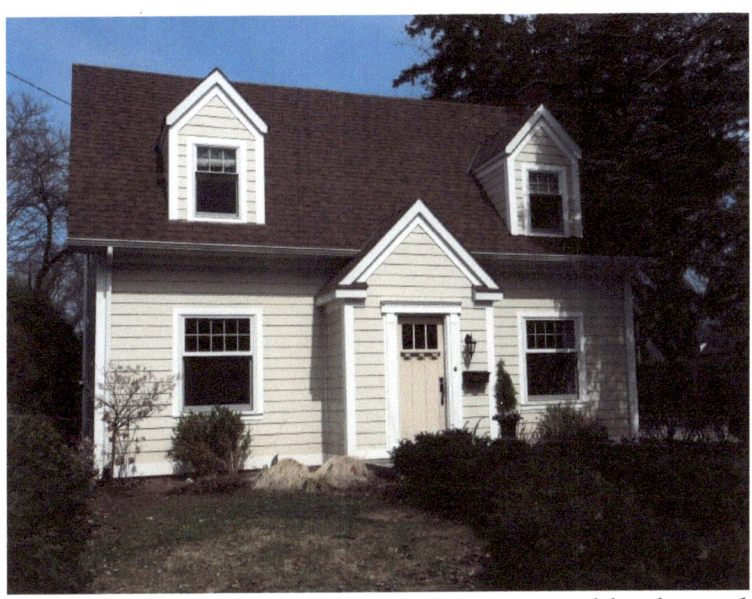

Hurd Avenue – dormers, cornice return on gable above door

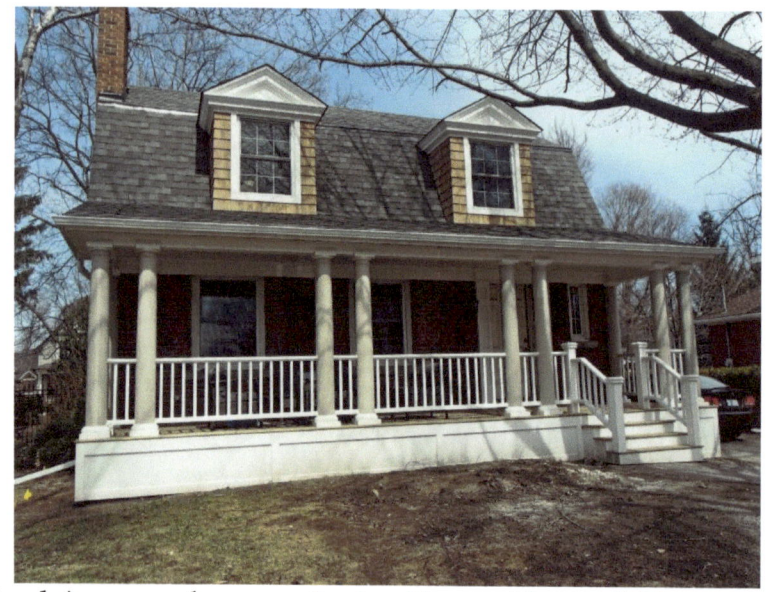

Hurd Avenue dormers, Ionic pillars with scroll-like capitals

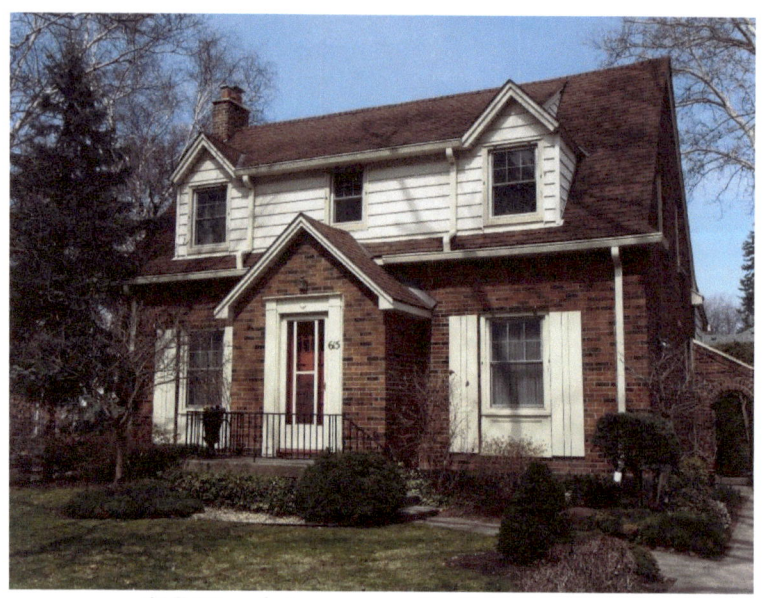

615 Hurd Avenue – Gothic Revival

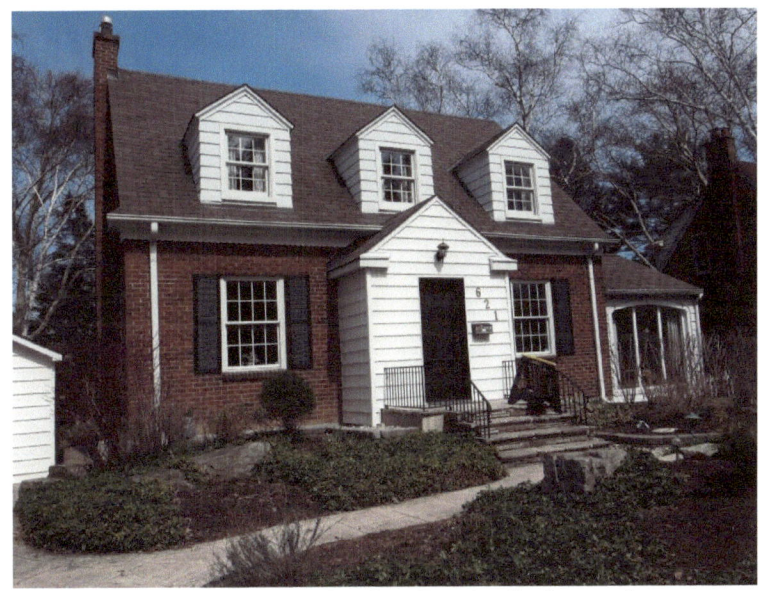

621 Hurd Avenue – Gothic Revival, three dormers

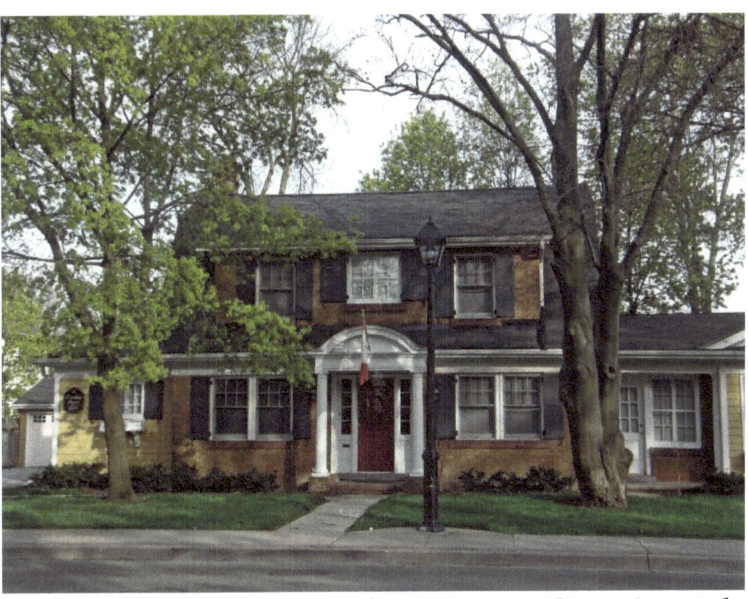

2080 Caroline Street - Caroline House – Georgian style

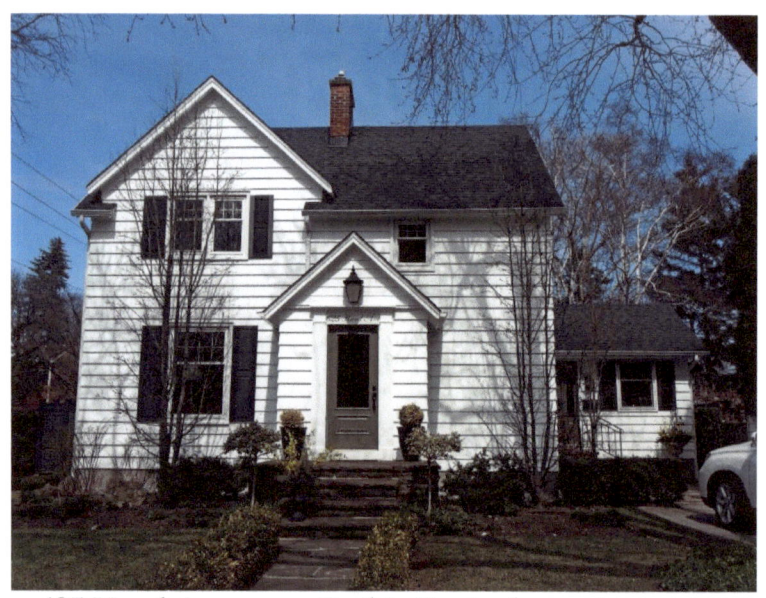

625 Hurd Avenue – Gothic Revival, cornice return

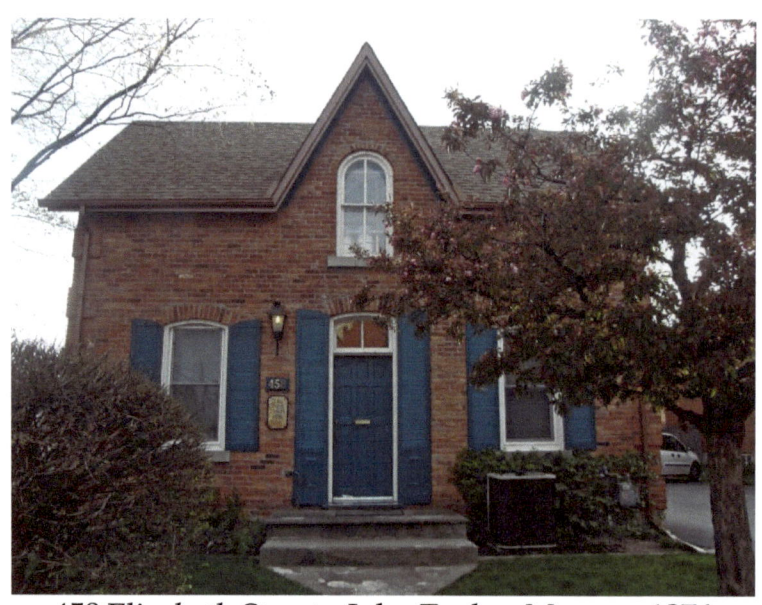

458 Elizabeth Street - John Taylor, Mason – 1876
Gothic Revival

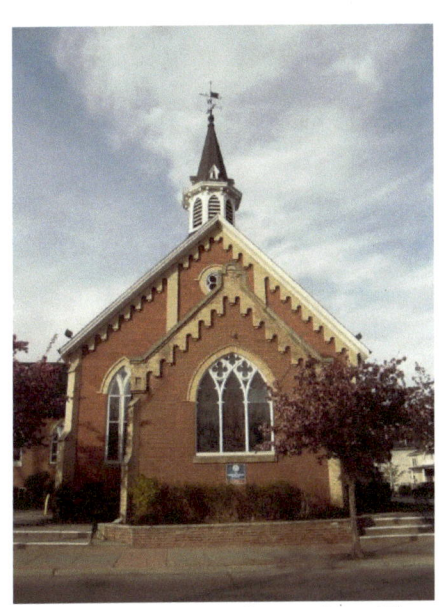

461 Elizabeth Street - Knox Presbyterian Church - 1845-1877

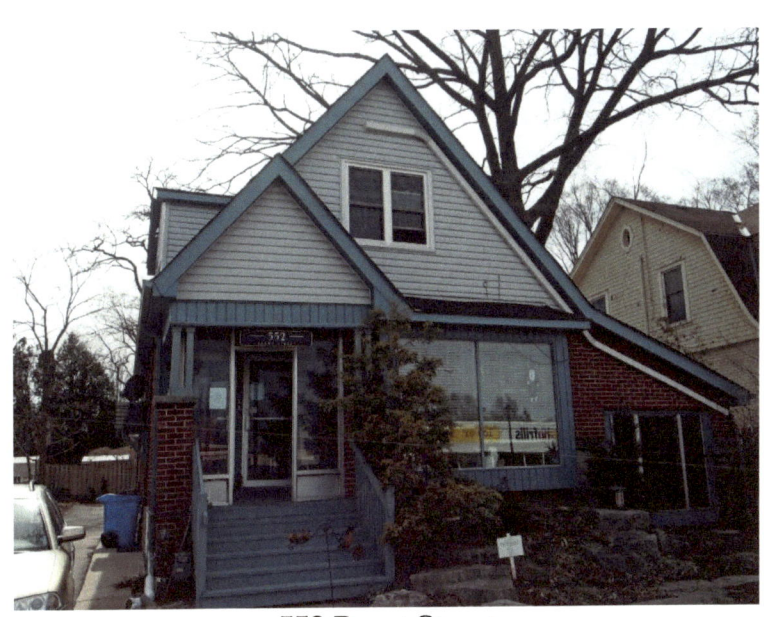

552 Brant Street

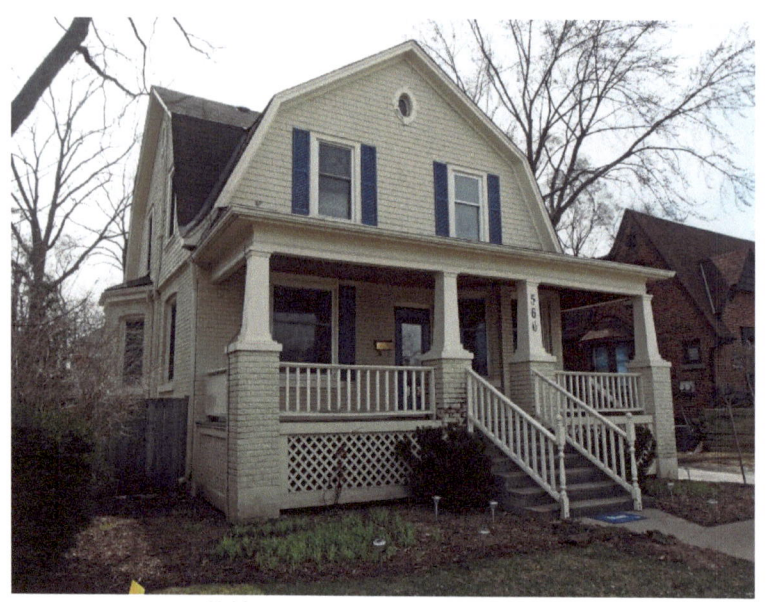

560 Brant Street – Gothic Revival

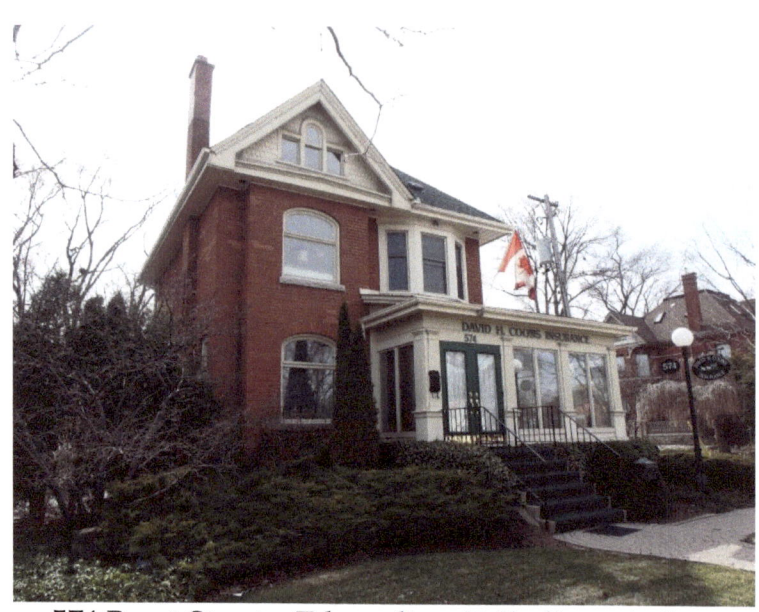

574 Brant Street – Edwardian, Palladian window

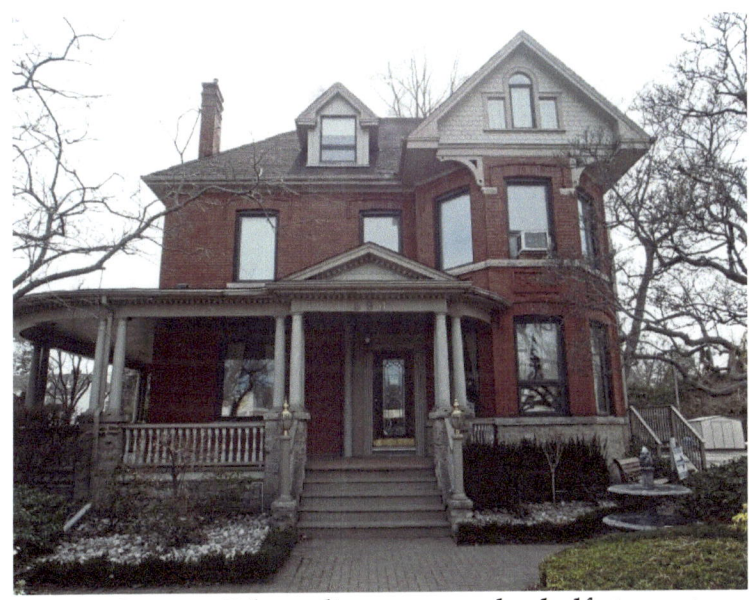

590 Brant Street – Edwardian, two-and-a-half storey tower-like bay with Palladian window, dormer in attic, pediment above wrap-around verandah

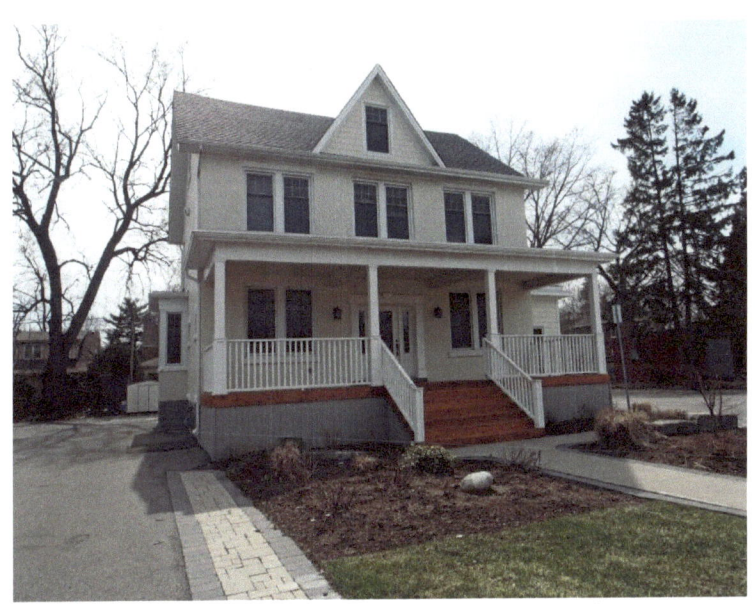

600 Brant Street – Gothic Revival

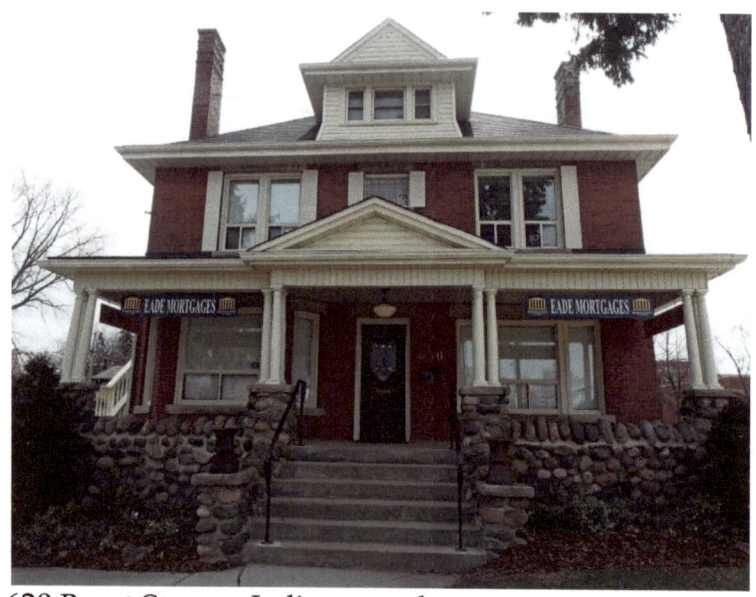

620 Brant Street – Italianate – dormer in attic, pediment

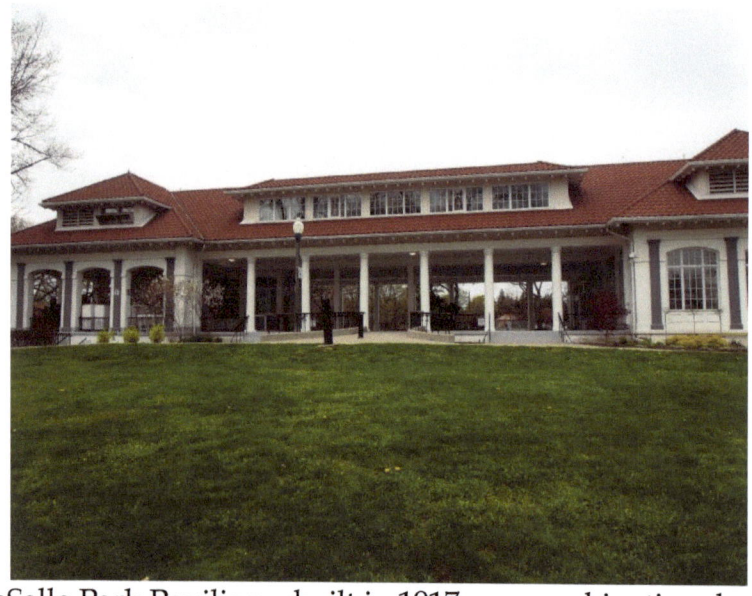

LaSalle Park Pavilion – built in 1917 as a combination dance and picnic pavilion with open verandah set between two arcaded pavilions decorated with pilasters – Art Deco style

Architectural Terms

Brackets: a decorative or weight-bearing structural element which forms a right angle with one side against a wall and the other under a projecting surface such as an eave or roof. Example: 2222 Lakeshore Road	
Cobblestone architecture: Refers to the use of cobblestones embedded in mortar as a method for erecting walls on houses and commercial buildings. Example: 558 Burlington Avenue	
Cornice: originally the wooden overhang of the roof. With the use of stone, brick, iron and steel, the cornice is any projecting shelf at the top of a ceiling or roof. They can be very decorative. Example: 479 Burlington Street	
Cornice Return: decorative element on the end of a gable. Example: 1401 Ontario Street	
Dichromatic brickwork: the use of two colours of brick, tile or slate to decorate a façade. Example: 472 Locust Street	
Dormer: (French for "sleep") a gable end window that pierces through the plane of a sloping roof surface to create usable space in the top floor or attic of a building by adding headroom. Example: 597 Locust Street	

Finial: ornament added to the top of a gable, pinnacle, canopy or spire – a Gothic element. Example: 551 Hurd Avenue	
Gable: the triangular portion of a wall between the edges of a sloping roof. Example: 2222 Lakeshore Road	
Hipped Roof: a roof where all sides slope downwards to the walls with no gables. Example: 561 Locust Street	
Lancet Window: a tall, narrow window with a pointed arch at its top. Example: 472 Locust Street	
Palladian Window: a large window that is divided into three sections with the centre section larger than the two side sections and usually arched. Example: 1413 Ontario Street	
Pediment: a triangular section above the horizontal structure (entablature), typically supported by columns. The inside of the triangle is called the tympanum. Example: 465 Burlington Street	

Quoin: masonry blocks at the corner of a wall, often a decorative feature, usually larger or of a different colour than the rest of the wall. Example: 2201 Lakeshore Road	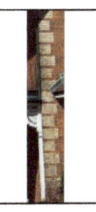
Vergeboards: also called bargeboards – hang from the projecting end of a roof and are often elaborately carved and ornamented. Example: 387 Lakeshore Road	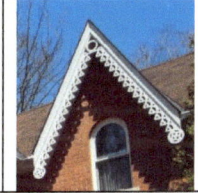

The Art Deco style was first developed for the French luxury market after World War I. The style was a self-conscious split from the past, the world before the war, and was designed to celebrate the new technologies of electricity and gas-powered vehicles. Art Deco left its mark on everything from lamps and foot stools to purses and hair combs. The design motifs are drawn from Ancient Egypt, Africa, Turkey, and Japan. The colours are influenced by the Fauves and the Cubists. The style was adopted in Ontario by wealthy and very fashionable patrons who wanted Art Deco detailing to make their buildings look lavish and exotic. Example: LaSalle Park Pavilion	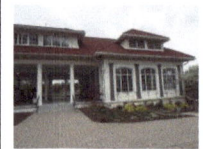
Edwardian, 1900-1930 – This style bridges the ornate and elaborate styles of the Victorian era and the simplified styles of the 20th century. Balanced facades, simple roof lines, dormer windows, large front porches, and smooth brick surfaces are its characteristics. Example: 1419 Ontario Street	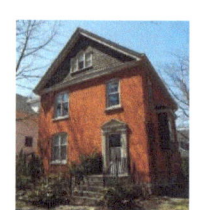
Georgian, before 1860 – This style began with the British King Georges in the 18th century. These buildings have balanced facades around a central door, medium-pitched gable roofs, and small paned windows. Example: 3050 Lakeshore Road	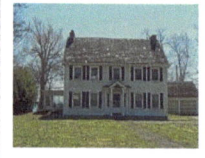

Gothic Revival, 1830-1890 – These decorative buildings have sharply-pitched gables with highly detailed vergeboards, pointed-arch window openings, and dichromatic brickwork. It is a common style in Ontario. Examples: 1401 Ontario Street	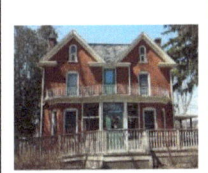
Italianate, 1850-1900 – It has wide-bracketed eaves, belvederes, wrap-around verandahs. Examples: 432 Smith Avenue	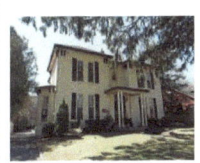
Queen Anne, 1885-1900 – This style is distinguished by an irregular outline featuring a combination of an offset tower, broad gables, projecting two-storey bays, verandahs, multi-sloped roofs, and tall, decorative chimneys. A mixture of brick and wood is common. Windows often have one large single-paned bottom sash and small panes in the upper sash. Example: Burlington Avenue	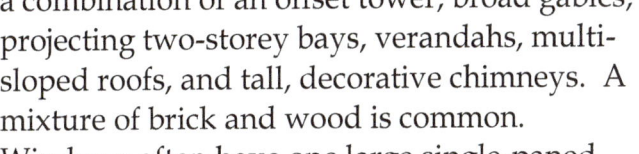
Regency Cottage, 1830-1860 – This style originated in England in 1815 and spread to Ontario later in the 19th century as British officers retired to Canada. It is a modest one-storey house with a low-pitched hip roof and has a symmetrical front façade. Example: 559 Burlington Avenue	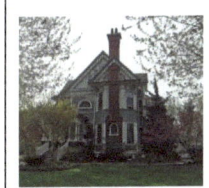
Tudor Revival – exposed timbers with stucco infill, multi-paned windows. Example: 3044 Lakeshore Road	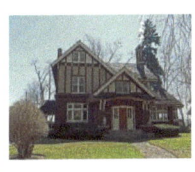

www.ingramcontent.com/pod-product-compliance
Lightning Source LLC
Chambersburg PA
CBHW040839180526
45159CB00001B/245